Fun Ideas
for family devotions

Mini-celebrations for families who care about each other and about God's plan for them

by
Ginger Jurries and Karen Mulder

 STANDARD PUBLISHING

Cincinnati, Ohio   2968

"Posterity will serve him; future generations will be told about the Lord."—Psalm 22:30, NIV

Unless otherwise specified, Scripture quotations are from the *New International Version* of the Bible, © 1979, New York Bible Society International.

Library of Congress Cataloging in Publication Data

Jurries, Ginger.
    Fun ideas for family devotions.

    1. Family—Prayer-books and devotions—
English.   I. Mulder, Karen.   II. Title.
BV255.J87   249   81-50347
ISBN 0-87239-415-8   AACR2

© 1981 The STANDARD PUBLISHING Company, Cincinnati, Ohio
A division of STANDEX INTERNATIONAL Corporation. Printed in U.S.A.

To Parents

Family Experience: This book is filled with learning experiences for the entire family. The content is particularly appropriate for families with children ages 5 to 10 years, but we believe that younger and older children will be drawn into the family fun time.

Fun Experience: We feel that having fun together while learning about God is as important as the concepts learned. Laughter and enthusiasm build family rapport, and lead to the forming of a positive attitude toward God.

Action: We learn by doing and discovering; therefore, the main focus of each family celebration is an activity. The varied activities are designed to lead to a meaningful discovery about self, others, and God.

Mini-Time: Quality rather than quantity of time is stressed. The average time required for each celebration is ten minutes.

Mini-Preparation: The family celebrations do not require lengthy preparations prior to the devotion time. A brief scanning of each day's content and materials is sufficient. The celebrations are developed in sequence. For this reason, we suggest that you start at the beginning and proceed from front to back.

Materials: Materials used in the various activities are usually common household items. We recommend that you start a family Treasure Chest. The Treasure Chest might include such things as construction paper, yarn, buttons, scraps of cloth, tinfoil, egg cartons, cardboard rolls, beads, glitter, greeting cards, pencils, felt-tip pens, crayons, glue, and tape.

If possible, each family member should have his/her own personal Bible. The Bibles should include both the Old and New Testaments.

—The Authors

Contents

UNIT IV

I Am Unique

UNIT V

My Power Source

Introduction

Let's Celebrate I Am Special!

Materials: A copy of this book, gift-wrapped
A 9 x 12 inch sheet of paper for each family member
Markers or crayons

FAMILY CELEBRATION: Let's get started!
1. Select, by having family members draw straws or guessing a number, someone to unwrap the book.
2. Ask each person to tell what pops into his/her mind when he thinks of celebrating.
3. Explain that this book will help you see how God made you the wonderful person you are. Each devotion is really a celebration.
4. Together look at random pages and talk about any that look especially interesting.
5. Point out that you will all be using the book together. Decide what time is the best to have your celebration each day.
6. Make origami houses by following the instructions.

Origami House

1. Fold a 9″ x 12″ piece of paper (not construction) in half crosswise. Hold it so that the fold is at the top.
2. Fold it again the other way.
3. Unfold.
4. Now fold each end to this crease, then unfold.
5. While holding ends open, fold down to form triangles at top.
6. Now for your artistic touch! With crayons or felt-tip pens, decorate the house with windows, doors, plants, etc., to make it look like your own house. Now draw yourself in the window. Proudly display your family's houses on a mantle or other prominent spot.

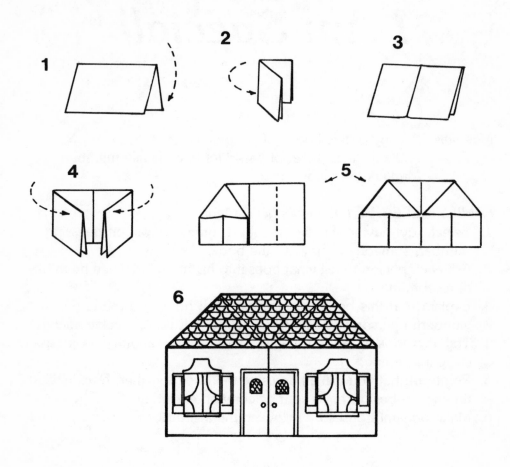

1

The Bible Is God's Word

MATERIALS: Gift-wrapped Bibles to be presented to each child as a
                  special gift
                  Activity sheet 1 (in the back of this book)
                  Pens or markers
                  Scissors
                  Cellophane tape
                  Song, "The B-I-B-L-E" (page 167)

BIBLE REFERENCE: 2 Timothy 3:16

FAMILY CELEBRATION
1. Unwrap the Bibles.
2. Read the Bible reference.
3. Sing together the song "The B-I-B-L-E."
4. Talk about what the song says about the Bible. Emphasize that the Bible is God's words to us.
5. Ask, "What does this verse say to you?"
6. Complete personal Bible bookplates by cutting out and filling in the bookplate on activity sheet 1. Tape bookplates to individual Bibles.
7. Use the words of Psalm 119:18 as a prayer: Dear God, open my eyes that I may see wonderful things in Your law. Amen.

2

The Bible Is God's Message to Me

MATERIALS: Bibles
Activity sheet 2
Pencils
Song, "The B-I-B-L-E" (page 167)

BIBLE REFERENCE: 2 Peter 1:21

FAMILY CELEBRATION
1. Using activity sheet 2, each family member solves the Bible puzzle.
2. Ask, "What does it say?"
3. Look up the Bible reference.
4. Ask, "What does this verse say?"
5. Sing "The B-I-B-L-E."

3

The Bible Is God's Love Letter to Me

MATERIALS: Song, "Jesus Loves Me" (page 167)
Bibles
Rectangular sheets of paper
Pencils or felt-tip pens

BIBLE REFERENCE: John 3:16

FAMILY CELEBRATION
1. Read John 3:16 from your Bibles.
2. Ask, "What do these Bible messages tell us about God?" (He LOVES us!)
3. Say, "The Bible is a love letter to us from God."
4. Each person writes a special Love Note to someone. (Smaller children may draw pictures instead of writing.)
5. When the Love Notes are finished, show family members how to fold them. (Directions on next page)
6. Talk about how the person who receives the note might feel when he reads it. What would happen if the person never took the time to read the Love Note? What would happen if we never read the *Bible?*
7. Mail or give the Love Notes to the proper persons.
8. Sing together "Jesus Loves Me."

Folding Love Notes

Fold your Love Note in half lengthwise.

Fold it again lengthwise.

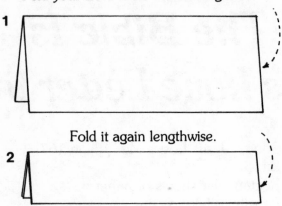

Fold the right ⅔ down.

Fold A back so that it is parallel to B.

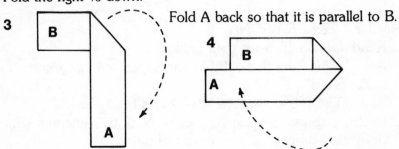

Fold A straight up, to form an "envelope" look, and slip behind section B.

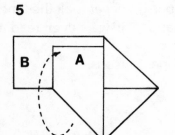

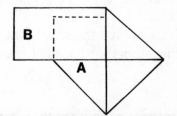

4

The Bible Is for Me to Use

MATERIALS: Bibles
Buttons or similar objects
Game "I Can Find It!" (activity sheet 3)

BIBLE REFERENCE: Ephesians 3:17

FAMILY CELEBRATION
1. Play the game, "I Can Find It."
   Game Objective: Each child successfully fulfills the requirements of each box and finally arrives at the last square, "I DID IT!" Everyone wins if everyone is able to finish and sign his name in the last box. (It may be necessary for parents to assist children when they need help and to check "findings." When the child gets the parents' "OK," the child may move his marker (button) to the next square.
2. Talk about why the Bible is an important book.
3. Read Ephesians 3:17.

5

God Designed Me

MATERIALS: Bibles
Activity sheet 4
Crayons or felt-tip pens
Buttons, yarn (optional)

BIBLE REFERENCE: Genesis 1:26, 27, 31

FAMILY CELEBRATION
1. Read the Bible reference.
2. Ask, "How did God feel about the man and woman He had designed?"
3. Give each member of the family a paper doll and outfit (activity sheet 4). Each family member should color in the features of the doll to look like himself or herself. Hair may be added by using yarn. Design the outfit any way you wish (buttons, etc., may be added).
4. Each family member thanks God in his own way for designing him just the way he is.

6

God Made Me

MATERIALS: Bibles

One object made by each family member: picture, clay
object, birdhouse, decoration, etc.

Activity sheet 5

Construction paper

BIBLE REFERENCE: Psalm 100:3

FAMILY CELEBRATION

1. Inquire about the ownership of each item.
2. Ask, "Why do you say that it belongs to you?"
3. Read the Bible reference. Ask, "To whom do you belong? Why?"
   Emphasize the fact that we belong to God because He made us.
4. Fill in Certificates of Ownership (activity sheet 5), and mount them
   on construction paper. Each child may hang his certificate in his
   room.
5. Pray that you will always remember that you belong to God.

7

God Made Me and He Bought Me

MATERIALS: Bibles
Activity sheet 6

FAMILY CELEBRATION
1. Read the following parable:

A Parable: Peter and His Sailboat

One day a little boy named Peter, who was nine years old, built a sailboat with wood and nails. He made a sail from a piece of an old sheet, and fastened it to a stick. Then he asked his father to drill a hole in the boat in which to poke the mast. It was now ready to sail—except for one thing. He carefully carved his initials on the bottom of his beautiful sailboat so that everyone would know that the boat belonged to him.

Peter was very excited as he launched his little boat in the stream near his house. His father ran beside him as they watched the small craft floating down the fast current. Suddenly the fun ceased when the wind began forcing the boat more rapidly down the river. The boy tried to rescue his precious sailboat, but the stiff September breeze was too much of a challenge for the tiny boat, and soon it was out of sight. What a great disappointment the boy felt! He loved the boat so very much.

Months passed. One day, as the boy was walking downtown, he passed a secondhand store. To his great surprise and delight, what should he see in the store window but his very own lost sailboat! Excitedly, he told the storekeeper that the boat in the window, the one with the sail, belonged to him! The storekeeper did not seem to understand or care about the boy's prize possession. Very calmly he said,

"All I know is that a much larger boy brought the boat to my shop several weeks ago saying that he had found it downstream."

"But it's mine," pleaded the boy. "Look at the bottom and you'll see my initials!"

Sure enough, there on the underside of the boat were the initials, P.D.M.

"I'm sorry, boy," said the man, "but this boat is for sale. If you want it you'll have to buy it. One dollar and fifty cents is the price."

As quickly as his legs could carry him, the boy bounded out the door and down the street. Once in his room he poured from his piggy bank pennies, nickels, and dimes. Eagerly he counted out the amount. One dollar and fifty cents was all he had, but suddenly he didn't care about spending it on anything else. Nothing mattered but getting back his sailboat.

Stuffing the money into his pocket, he raced back downtown on his bike.

"I've come to buy my boat!" Peter eagerly proclaimed to the storekeeper!

Holding it in his arms, Peter spoke to the little boat as if to a long lost friend.

"Little boat," he said, "now you are twice mine. First I made you, and now I bought you."

2. Each family member cuts his activity sheet 6 apart.
3. First, arrange the sequence with the boy and the sailboat in the right order. Have one child briefly tell the three main events from this story. (Main point is on the back of each card.)
4. Say, "This is a parable because it has an earthly and a heavenly meaning." Now, using the other picture cards, tell the story with the heavenly meaning. (The Bible reference clue is on the back of each card.)
5. Thank God for buying us back with the highest price He could have paid, the blood of His Son Jesus.

8

God Loves Me, Always

MATERIALS: Bibles
Activity sheet 7
Pencils

BIBLE REFERENCE: John 3:16

FAMILY CELEBRATION
1. Ask, "What was the message of the parable, Peter and His Sailboat?" (God made me and showed His great love for me by sending Jesus Christ to be my Savior.)
2. Ask, "Does God love us every minute of every day?" "Does God love us even when we sin?"
3. Say, "Let's see what the Bible says about God's wonderful love." Use activity sheet 7 and decode the messages from God.
4. Talk about the meaning of the decoded verses.
5. Read or say together John 3:16.

9

God Loves Me Even When I Sin

MATERIALS: Bibles
Slips of paper
Pencils
Large metal pot placed in the sink

BIBLE REFERENCE: Matthew 22:37, 38 and 1 John 1:9

FAMILY CELEBRATION
1. Read Matthew 22:37 and 38.
2. Ask, "What did Jesus say is the greatest commandment?" Have each family member think of one thing he or she has done in the past few days which does not follow this commandment.
3. Have each family member write that sin on a piece of paper. (Younger children may draw a picture.) Tell the children that they do not have to tell this sin to the other family members.
4. Read 1 John 1:9. Each family member audibly confesses that he has sinned and asks for forgiveness.
5. Put all the slips of paper into the metal pot or fireplace and burn them.
6. Explain that when we are sorry for our sins and tell God that we are sorry, He forgives us and takes them away just as surely as the slips of paper are gone.

10

God Says
I Am Special

MATERIALS: Bibles
Paper
Crayons or felt-tip pens

BIBLE REFERENCE: Isaiah 43:1b

FAMILY CELEBRATION
1. Read the Bible reference. Each person tells what the verse means to him/her.
2. Tell the children that God thinks they are very special and that you do, too.
3. With crayons, each family member prints his name in large letters, then outlines the letters several times using a different color each time. See the samples on the next page.
4. Say the Bible verse together. Encourage everyone to memorize this verse.

11

God's Grand Plan for Moses

MATERIALS: Paper, pencils, crayons, poster board
Moses puzzle (page 23)
Narrative for Moses puzzle (page 25)

Note to Parents: This celebration may be divided into two days. A suggested stopping point for the first day is at the end of puzzle piece number 7.

FAMILY CELEBRATION
1. Glue the puzzle pictures (page 23) onto poster board. Weight the pictures down with books until dry, then cut out each piece.
2. Ask, "Did you know that God has a Grand Plan for your life?" "What do you think Grand Plan means?"
3. "Today we are going to discover God's Grand Plan for a man named Moses."
4. Procedure for putting puzzle together: Say, "I will read some information. Every time I stop, you will find the puzzle piece that goes with the information. Put each new piece next to the last piece."
5. After the puzzle is completed, talk about how each puzzle piece (part of Moses' life) was an important part of God's plan for Moses.
6. Close with a chain prayer, in which each family member thanks God for one thing.

Narrative for Moses Puzzle

Note to Reader: Read each puzzle piece information starting with number 1. Stop at the end of each puzzle piece and allow the family to locate the proper piece and put it in position.

Puzzle Piece #1: Look for a group of people with unhappy faces. Why do they look so sad? They're sad because they are slaves in a country called Egypt. They cannot choose where they will live or what type of work they will do. The man with the long whip is an Egyptian. He wants the slaves to work harder.

Puzzle Piece #2: The evil ruler of Egypt made all the slaves work very hard. He also commanded that all the baby boys born to the slaves should be killed. One mother hid her baby boy in a little basket-boat. The baby's name was Moses.

Puzzle Piece #3: God had a grand plan for Moses' life, and He did not allow Moses to be killed. In this picture, baby Moses is being rescued from the basket-boat by a pretty Egyptian princess. She loves the baby, and when Moses becomes older he will live with her in the palace. Until then, she asks Moses' own mother to take care of him. (The princess did not know that the lady was Moses' real mother.)

Puzzle Piece #4: Moses, in this picture, is living with the pretty Egyptian princess in the palace. Look at his fancy clothes! Moses learned many things while he lived in the palace. He learned how to be a soldier; he also probably studied sports, art, writing, music, math, reading, law, the stars and planets, medicine, and the teachings of many great men.

Puzzle Piece #5: Even though Moses was rich and was a prince, he never forgot his family and neighbors who were still slaves. When he went riding in his chariot, he often stopped to watch the slaves as they pulled heavy stones under the hot sun. One day while Moses was watching the slaves work, he saw a slave being beaten by an Egyptian boss. Moses became so angry that he killed the Egyptian.

Puzzle Piece #6: When the Egyptian ruler, the Pharaoh, heard what Moses had done, he said that Moses must be killed. But Moses ran away to a land called Midian.

Puzzle Piece #7: Moses lived in this wilderness for forty years. He lived with a man named Jethro. After awhile, Moses married Jethro's daughter. Moses' job was taking care of the family's sheep. As he sat on the hills, watching the sheep, Moses often thought about his people far away in Egypt. He thought about how they had to be slaves and work so hard. (You may stop here and continue at next celebration time)

Puzzle Piece #8: One day, while Moses was watching the sheep, he saw a bush burning. It kept burning, but it wasn't destroyed. God told Moses that he must go back to Egypt and lead the slaves to freedom.

Puzzle Piece #9: Eighty-year-old Moses went back to Egypt, and in this puzzle piece he is trying to convince the Pharaoh of Egypt to free the slaves. The Pharaoh says, "No!"

Puzzle Piece #10: Because the Pharaoh would not listen to Moses, God made terrible things happen to the Egyptian people. These terrible things were called plagues. Can you tell me about some of these plagues? (If you would like to read about the plagues, you can find them in Exodus, chapters 7-11.)

Puzzle Piece #11: The Egyptian Pharaoh finally got so angry, because of the terrible plagues, that he ordered all the slaves to leave Egypt. In this picture, Moses is the leader for about 600,000 people. The people are called Israelites. The Israelites are leaving Egypt and are no longer slaves. How would you like to be the leader of 600,000 people?

Puzzle Piece #12: God promised these people a special country in which to live, a country that would be their own. They traveled for forty years in the wilderness (desert). Moses, guided and directed by God, provided food, water, laws and rules, protection and guidance for all those people for forty years.

Puzzle Piece #13: As their leader, Moses was always very busy. God would tell Moses what the Israelites should do, then Moses would teach the people. In this picture, God has given Moses ten important laws to help make life happier and more peaceful. These laws were for the Israelites and they are also for us. They are called the Ten Commandments.

Puzzle Piece #14: Moses also spent time writing down all that happened to the Israelites, so that we can learn from their experiences. Find in your Bible the books that Moses wrote: Genesis, Exodus, Leviticus, Numbers, and Deuteronomy.

Puzzle Piece #15: God certainly did have a Grand Plan for Moses' life. In Deuteronomy 34:7, 10, 11, we read, "Moses was a hundred and twenty years old when he died, yet his eyes were not weak nor his strength gone. . . . Since then, no prophet has risen in Israel like Moses, whom the Lord knew face to face, who did all those miraculous signs and wonders the Lord sent him to do. . . ."

12

God Has a Grand Plan for My Life

MATERIALS: A puzzle (preferably one the family hasn't put together previously)

FAMILY CELEBRATION
1. Ask, "What was the Grand Plan God had for Moses' life?" Select two or three of the puzzle pieces you used in the previous family celebration and ask, "In what way was the experience on this puzzle piece part of God's plan for Moses?"
2. Say, "God also has a Grand Plan for your life."
3. Place the puzzle pieces you plan to put together today face up, on the table. (Do not let anyone see the picture of the finished puzzle.)
4. Ask, "How is this puzzle like our lives?"
5. As you put the puzzle together, talk about some of the things God is accomplishing in your lives. (If you have chosen a large puzzle, you may want to divide this activity into several days.)
6. Read Proverbs 3:5, 6.

13

God Gave Me a Family

MATERIALS: Bibles

Cakes or cupcakes with birthday candles (a surprise!)

BIBLE REFERENCE: Psalm 127:3

FAMILY CELEBRATION

1. Read the Bible reference.
2. Parents sing "You're a Blessing to Us" ("Happy Birthday" tune) to children while presenting birthday cake.

    "You're a Blessing to Us"

    You're a blessing to us.

    You're a blessing to us.

    You're a blessing, dear   (name)

    You're a blessing to us!
3. All the children may blow out the candles together.
4. Eat and celebrate!
5. While eating the cake, parents should talk about some events that occurred on the days the children were born or when they were very young. Tell the children how happy you were when they finally "arrived."
6. Have each person thank God for the family member to his right.

14

My Family Thinks I Am Special

MATERIALS: Bibles
Copies of children's birth certificates
Baby items such as birth bracelets, pictures, cards, etc.
Tape measure or ruler
Song, "You're Something Special" (page 169)
(Optional items) Paper, pencils, thread, stick or dowel

BIBLE REFERENCE: Psalm 127:3

FAMILY CELEBRATION
1. Read the Bible reference.
2. Show and talk about each child's birth certificate and other baby items. Be sure to include snapshots if you have them.
3. Have fun measuring first day footprints and compare them with the size of the children's feet today. Then compare baby height with present height.
4. Tell your children how glad you are that they are yours.
5. (Optional) Make an outline of one foot by tracing it. Cut out and make a mobile of family members' feet. Be sure to write names on footprints, identifying them.
6. Sing "You're Something Special" together.

15

My Family Needs Me

MATERIALS: Bibles
Song, "You're Something Special" (page 169)
Activity sheet 8

FAMILY CELEBRATION
1. Read together verse three of song. Talk about the line in the verse that says, *"And each one needs the other to help him through the day."*
2. Sing "You're Something Special."
3. Complete activity sheet 8. (Each person fills in the blanks on his /her activity sheet. Younger children will need help.)
4. Each person shares what he wrote in each blank.
5. Make a family circle by holding hands. One family member starts and says to the person on his left, "I am so glad, (name) , that you are a member of the (family's last name) family."
(Forming a "family circle" by joining hands during prayer or singing could be a new, meaningful tradition to start in your family.)

16

Mom and Dad Love Me—No "Ifs"

MATERIALS: Bibles
Paper
Crayons or markers

BIBLE REFERENCE: John 15:17

FAMILY CELEBRATION
1. Pass out paper and crayons, and tell each family member to draw a picture of something that he/she wants to accomplish (twirl a baton, fly an airplane, etc.).
2. Read the Bible reference.
3. Ask, "Did Jesus say to love a person IF he or she does nice things, or IF he or she is a good swimmer or gets all super marks in school?" (You may want to add accomplishments family members have drawn on their papers.)
4. Ask, "What did Jesus command?" (To love one another without any "ifs.")
5. Family members "show and tell" about the accomplishment drawn on their papers. Parents after hearing individual goals, emphasize, "We will be very excited and happy when you accomplish this goal. *But, we love you even if you do not.*"
6. Ask for a volunteer to say a short prayer.

17

Mom and Dad Love Me, Always

MATERIALS: Play money or pieces of paper
Desk or table, chair
"Robe" (sheet, curtain, jacket, etc.)
Ring
Cane or stick
A lively song on record or tape
Script, "The Prodigal Son" (page 33)

FAMILY CELEBRATION
1. Act out the drama of "The Prodigal Son." (Assign appropriate parts with a parent or older child taking the part of the narrator.)
2. Ask, "Why didn't the father scold his son when he came back home? Do you think he loved his son even though he had been selfish?"
3. Tell the children that you love them and always will, no matter what bad things they might do.
4. Family members hold hands and the parents say, "I love you when you make me glad! I love you when you make me sad! I always will love you!" Thank God for the love you have for one another.

Drama: The Prodigal Son

Actors needed: narrator, wayward son, father, pig(s), servant(s). (Family members may take more than one part or more than one member may play the parts of servants and pigs.)

Props needed: play money or pieces of paper, desk or table, chair, "robe" (curtain, sheet, jacket, etc.), ring, cane or stick, record player or tape player, a lively song on tape or record.

Act 1

Actors: narrator, father, son
Props: play money
NARRATOR: There once was a father who had two sons. The father was very wealthy. The younger son longed for adventure. *(SON enters.)* One day the son came to his father and said, "I'd rather have my share of your money now than after you die, Father." The father didn't even ask what he would do with it. He just gave it to him. *(FATHER takes a large roll or stack of money from his drawer and gives it to the son. The SON skips merrily away—into the next room.)*

Act 2

Actors: narrator, father
Props: cane or stick, desk, chair
(FATHER sits at his desk or table.)
NARRATOR: Every day the father went to look for the son, hoping that he would come home again.
(FATHER goes to the doorway, using his cane as he walks, and looks into the distance. He then walks sadly back and sits down again.)

Act 3

Actors: narrator, son, pigs
Props: "money"
(The SON comes in with a stack of money.)
NARRATOR: The son had a good time spending all his father's money. It didn't take very long before it was all gone.
(SON merrily throws the money into the air.)

The son hadn't thought at all about the future. Soon a famine came to the land where the son was living. The son was starving, and had to go to work for a farmer.

(PIGS enter, snort, and pretend to be eating. The SON sits down next to the pigs.)

NARRATOR: One day the son noticed the pigs. They were fat and well fed. Even the garbage they were eating looked good to him. Suddenly he realized how foolish he had been. He thought for a while. *(SON scratches his head, pretending to be thinking.)* He decided what he would do. He would go home and ask his father to forgive him and make him one of his servants. He didn't even feel special enough to be called a son any longer. *(SON gets up and begins to walk quickly home.)*

Act 4

Actors: narrator, father, son, servant

Props: "robe," ring, record or tape, recorder

(Enter FATHER, looking for SON, then running to greet him.)

NARRATOR: Before the son even gets near his home, the father sees him and runs to greet him. The son begins to ask for forgiveness but the father has already forgiven him in his heart. He is too happy to have him home to even scold him. *(FATHER hugs and kisses SON.)* He tells his servant to get the best robe and a ring. *(SERVANT brings them to the FATHER who puts them on the SON.)* Then they have a big party to celebrate the son's return. *(All join hands and skip in a circle to music.)*

The End

18

I Am Special!

MATERIALS: Song, "You're Something Special" (page 169)

FAMILY CELEBRATION
1. Sing verse one of "You're Something Special."
2. Talk about gestures and movements that could be used to express the ideas of the verse.
3. Sing verse one again. Add your action! (gestures and movements) Have fun—laughing is acceptable!
4. Continue above procedure for the other verses. (Stop when children lose interest.)
5. Ask a family member to say a short prayer of thanks for each individual.

19
I Am Wonderfully Made

MATERIALS: Bibles

(Optional) Book showing internal and external parts of the body

BIBLE REFERENCE: Psalm 139:13, 14

FAMILY CELEBRATION

1. Read the Bible reference. Talk about what the verses say about each of us.
2. (Optional) Look at pictures of the human body. Read interesting information about some of the parts of our wonderful bodies.
3. Play "I'm Thinking of a Wonderful Part of My Body."
   a. One family member starts the game by keeping in mind one of the parts of his body.
   b. He says to the rest of the family, "I'm thinking of a wonderful part of my body. What is it?"
   c. Each family member asks one question to gain information about the body part.
   d. The family members guess what body part it could be until one of them guesses correctly. (The family may need to set a time limit.)
   e. Each family member has a turn being "it."
4. Read the facts contained on page 37.
5. "God, thank You for giving each one of us a wonderful body. Amen."

Interesting Facts About Your Body

Your brain is the most complex structure in the universe. It weighs three pounds and contains 13,000,000,000 nerve cells. These cells store every sound, action, smell, and taste you have ever experienced!

A good head of hair is so strong it can support more than 2,000 pounds, equal to the weight of a large horse!

Each hand has 27 small bones. Together, the hands have over 54 bones, over one-fourth of the 206 bones in the whole body!

Within your five quarts of blood are twenty-two trillion blood cells. Each second, two million of your blood cells die to be replaced by two million new cells!

Your heart pumps blood through more than 60,000 miles of veins, arteries, and tubing each year!

You have as many miles of blood vessels in your body as there are miles of railroad tracks in the USA!

Your intestines are a tube that is about thirty feet long. Measure a distance of thirty feet with a yardstick to see what a great distance that is.

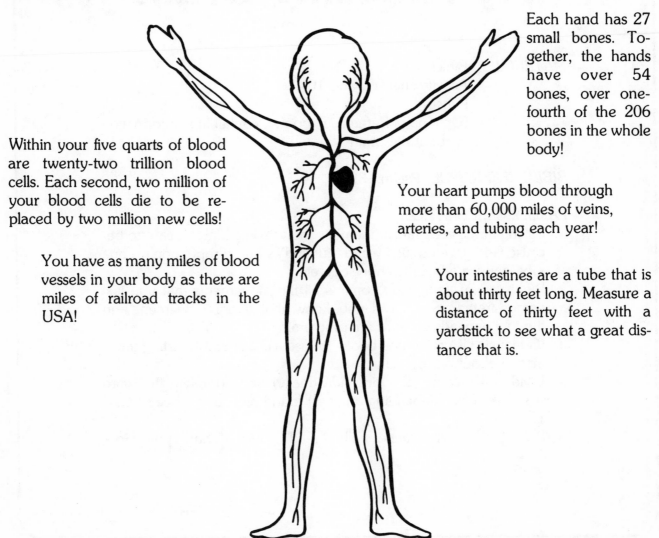

20

My Amazing Brain

MATERIALS: Bibles
Activity sheets 9 and 10
Pencils
(Optional) Reference books containing information about the brain

BIBLE REFERENCE: Psalm 139:13, 14

FAMILY CELEBRATION
1. Taking turns, each family member shows something he can do because God gave us such wonderful bodies (jump rope, hop on one foot, bounce a ball, tie shoelaces, etc.).
2. What part of your body controls all the movements that you just demonstrated? Say, "Did you know that every movement and thought depends on your amazing brain?"
3. (Optional) Use reference books to discover some interesting information about our brains.
4. Divide into teams (or work individually) and complete the word search or maze (depending on ages) found on activity sheets 9 and 10.
5. Read the Bible reference. Follow reading with "Thank you, God. Amen."

21

I Have an Amazing Brain: I Can Remember

MATERIALS: Bibles

Bag containing about 12 assorted objects (comb, pencil, candle, thread, etc.)

Paper and pencil for each family member

Activity sheet 11

BIBLE REFERENCE: Psalm 119:11

FAMILY CELEBRATION

1. Recall together what the family talked about during last session.
2. Say, "One very important function of the brain is memory. Can you give reasons why our ability to remember is so important?"
3. Play this memory game: Spread the objects from the bag onto the table. Give everyone thirty seconds to observe them. When the time is up, put the objects back into the bag. Give each person a paper and pencil and allow him one minute to write down each remembered object. Preschoolers may draw the objects. The family member recalling the most correct objects gets to choose tomorrow night's dessert (or other suitable reward).
4. Read the Bible reference. Ask, "How do you store words in your heart? Do you think it is important to memorize Bible verses? Why?"
5. (Optional) Learn one ABC verse a day (activity sheet 11). Hang the sheets where the children will be likely to see them often. Reward when all verses are memorized.
6. Thank God for your amazing memory.

22

I Have an Amazing Brain: I Can Imagine

MATERIALS: Bibles
Construction paper
Pencils
Crayons or markers
Rulers
Activity sheet 12 (on back of 7)

BIBLE REFERENCE: 1 Samuel 17:17-53

FAMILY CELEBRATION
1. Look up the word *imagination* in the dictionary. Ask, "What kinds of things can you do because of your ability to imagine?"
2. Say, "I am going to read the story about David and Goliath. When I am finished, we will draw the pictures that we saw in our minds." Read the Bible reference.
3. Pass out activity sheets and pencils. Say that we are going to make a comic strip about our story by drawing a picture in each square of the comic strip (see title above each box). Color the pictures with crayons or markers. Cut strips and tape together. Display on construction paper.
4. Show and tell your strip to the rest of the family.
5. Ask God to help you to use your wonderful imagination to become a better person for Him.

23

I Have an Amazing Brain: I Can Learn

MATERIALS: Bible
Song, "The Twelve Apostles" (page 173)

BIBLE REFERENCE: Luke 2:41-47

FAMILY CELEBRATION
1. Read the Bible reference. Ask, "How did Jesus learn?" (listening, discussing, asking questions)
2. Say, "Today we are going to learn the names of Jesus' apostles (special friends) by singing a song." With parental help, learn the song, "The Twelve Apostles." Sing together several times.
3. See how many apostles each family member can name.
4. Thank God for your amazing brain that helps you to learn things easily.

24

I Have an Amazing Brain: I Can Create

MATERIALS: Bibles

Purchased *Play-Doh,* your own play dough (see recipe on next page), or building toy such as *Legos*

BIBLE REFERENCE: Revelation 4:11

FAMILY CELEBRATION

1. Read the Bible reference. Together name some of the things that God created.
2. Ask, "What is the meaning of the word *create?*" (Look up the word in the dictionary.) Ask, "Can we create?" (Yes, we can make things by using our amazing brains and the materials that God has created.)
3. Ask the family to give examples of things man can "create." (Stories, poems, drawings, new machines, toys, recipes, etc.)
4. Create something new. Give each family member a portion of *Play-doh* (or *Legos*) and create something new (toy, vase, decoration, machine, building, etc.).
5. Each person "shows and tells" his creation.
6. Read Isaiah 64:8.

> O Lord, you are our Father.
> We are the clay, you are the potter;
> we are all the work of your hand.
>   Amen.

Play Dough Recipe

1 cup flour
½ cup salt
2 T. cream of tartar
1 T. cooking oil or baby oil
1 cup water

Mix together in heavy pan, stirring over medium heat until mixture pulls away from the side of the pan. (It will be gloppy and lumpy.)
Knead.
Add food coloring.
Store in ziplock or plastic container.

25

I Have an Amazing Brain: I Have Feelings

MATERIALS: Bibles

Small slips of paper containing the words: proud, angry, disappointed, important, happy, sad, frightened, jealous, embarrassed, shy, ashamed

Medium or large sized balloons with "feeling" slips inserted into them and blown up, or slips folded and put into a container

Needle or pointed object

Song, "If You're Happy" (page 175)

BIBLE REFERENCE: Ecclesiastes 3:1-8

FAMILY CELEBRATION

1. Say, "I am going to read some Bible verses, and every time you hear words that describe a feeling, stop me and say the name of the feeling."
2. Read the Bible reference.
3. Give each person one or more balloons. Taking turns (a parent should take the first turn), each person pops the balloon, discovers the slip of paper, reads the word on the paper, and says, "I remember a time when I felt (word on the paper)." Then the person describes the situation and tells why he had that feeling.
4. Ask, "Did anyone have anything happen today that made him especially happy or sad?"
5. Sing together "If You're Happy," using variation. Thank God for specific happy times.

26

I Have an Amazing Brain: I Can Choose

MATERIALS: Bibles
Activity sheets 13 and 14
Pencils

BIBLE REFERENCE: Genesis 2:15-17 and Genesis 3:1-6

FAMILY CELEBRATION
1. Say, "God gave each one of us the ability to choose (make decisions). Listen to the following story about Adam and Eve and see if you can find an example of their making a choice."
2. Read the Bible references and talk about the above.
3. Say, "God gave each of us the ability to choose. Can you give an example of a choice you made today?" (Choices may be about clothes, food, free time, etc.)
4. Read Step 1 instructions on activity sheets 13 and 14. Each family member completes a sheet. (If you have younger children, this activity may be done orally.)

27

I Can Grow Physically

MATERIALS: Bibles
Paper, ruler, pencils, felt-tip pens

BIBLE REFERENCE: Luke 2:52

FAMILY CELEBRATION
1. Read the Bible reference.
2. Ask, "What were the three ways Jesus grew?" "What does the word *stature* mean?" "What does your body need in order to grow physically?" (Emphasize plenty of sleep, good food, and exercise.)
3. Make "I Am Growing Bigger" charts like the sample on page 48 and hang in appropriate spots. Measure each child's height; each child records his height on his chart. Fill in height for previous years if information is available.
4. Ask, "Why is exercise so important?"

5. Do some exercises together. (Choose exercises that your family would enjoy. Following are some suggestions.)
   a. *The Inch Worm:* Starting from a standing position, bend forward and place both hands on the floor. The feet are kept stationary while the hands walk forward as far as possible. Then the hands remain stationary while the feet walk forward to a position close to the hands. The cycle is then repeated.
   b. See who can *skip rope* the longest.
   c. *Limbo:* Each family member takes turns shuffling under a broom or stick by walking forward with the body bent backward at the waist. Anyone who touches the broom or falls is out of the game. Each time all family members have taken a turn, lower the broom about two inches. Repeat until only one person remains.
6. Each person checks the physical goals that he has already mastered. (The family might like to select one of the activities as a family goal to be worked on and accomplished.)
7. Choose a family member to read the poem-prayer:

> Thank You, God, for hands that catch,
> Feet that skip and play hopscotch.
> Help me, Lord, my whole life through
> To keep them strong and well for You.

I CAN GROW PHYSICALLY

___ 66"
___ 65"
___ 64"
___ 63"
___ 62"
___ 61"
___ 60" 5 FT.
___ 59"
___ 58"
___ 57"
___ 56"
___ 55"
___ 54"
___ 53"
___ 52"
___ 51"
___ 50"
___ 49"
___ 48" 4 FT.
___ 47"
___ 46"
___ 45"
___ 44"
___ 43"
___ 42"
___ 41"
___ 40"
___ 39"
___ 38"
___ 37"
___ 36" 3 FT.
___ 35"
___ 34"
___ 33"
___ 32"
___ 31"

CHECK THE SKILLS
YOU CAN DO

Climb a Tree ___
Ride a Bike ___
Run a Mile ___
Jump Rope 100 Times ___
Throw a Ball ___
Shoot a Basket ___
Hit a Softball ___
Swim 30 Feet ___
Ice Skate ___
Roller Skate ___
Play Tennis ___
Do 15 Push-ups ___
Front Roll ___
Do 5 Pull-ups ___
Jump Over Sawhorse ___
Catch a Frisbee ___
Broad Jump 3 Feet ___
Row a Boat ___
Skateboard ___
Cart Wheel ___

28
I Can Grow Mentally

MATERIALS: Bibles
Activity sheet 15
Pencils

BIBLE REFERENCE: Luke 2:52

FAMILY CELEBRATION
1. Read the Bible verse.
2. Talk about the meaning of the words, "Jesus grew in wisdom . . ."
3. Ask, "What are some of the things you could do during your first year of life?" (smile, crawl, cry, stand up, etc.)
4. Say, "Let's see if each one of us has grown mentally since our first birthday." Remove activity sheet 15. Check the mental skills each has learned. Add, in the blanks provided, any other skills he/she has learned.
5. Talk about how much everyone has grown mentally.
6. Ask, "How do you think you became smarter and able to do more mental skills?" (read, studied, listened, asked questions, etc.)
7. (Optional) Each family member chooses one new mental skill he would like to accomplish within a certain time period.
8. Ask God to help us remember to study and read so that we will continue to grow mentally.
9. Hang the activity sheets next to the "I Can Grow Physically" chart. Remember to check new skills when they are mastered.

29

I Can Grow Spiritually

MATERIALS: Bibles
Activity sheet 16
Felt-tip pens or crayons
Heavy thread

BIBLE REFERENCE: Luke 2:52

FAMILY CELEBRATION
1. Say, "Who can name two ways in which Jesus grew?" (Physically and mentally) Does anyone know a third way to grow? Read Luke 2:52 to check your answer. Say, "Gaining favor with God or pleasing God is the same thing as growing spiritually."
2. Ask, "What are some ways that we can grow spiritually?" (Read Bible, pray, go to church, follow Jesus' teachings, etc.)
3. Say, "We are each going to make a mobile for our rooms to remind us to grow spiritually."

4. Cut outlines from activity page. Add details with markers or crayons. Lay one of the church buildings on a flat surface. Two inches below it, lay the person outline. Two inches below that, lay the open Bible. Put a small amount of glue down the center of the three outlines. Cut about an 18″ length of thread. Lay it so that it follows the glue line, leaving about 6″ of thread at the top above the church building. Now place remaining cutouts on matching symbols.
5. Hang mobile in each family member's room. Read the verses that are printed on the mobile.
6. Tell the family members that in the next celebration we will have a "show time." Each member should prepare to display a skill to the rest of the family. This should be something that has been accomplished through practice: play an instrument, gymnastics, jump rope, write or read a poem, etc.

30

I Thank God for My Wonderful Body

PREPARATION: A "show time" activity, chosen by each family member (as assigned in last celebration)

FAMILY CELEBRATION
1. *Show Time:* Each family member "shows" the skill he has chosen to perform.
2. Say, "We were able to perform these activities because God gave us such wonderful bodies. How can we thank God for our wonderful bodies?" (After the family has responded to this question, read the following Indian prayer which also tells ways we can thank God for our bodies:)

An Indian Prayer

Let me walk in beauty, and make my eyes ever
behold the red and purple sunset.
Make my hands respect the things You have made,
and my ears sharp to hear Your voice.
Make me wise so that I may understand the things
You have taught my people.
Let me learn the lessons You have hidden in every
leaf and rock.

31

I Am Unique

MATERIALS: A child's collection (shells, rocks, stamps, etc.)
Magnifying glass (optional)
Bibles

BIBLE REFERENCE: Luke 12:6, 7

FAMILY CELEBRATION
1. Compare items of a collection.
2. Say, "Each one of these items is unique. What do you think that means?" (Stress the idea that unique means one-of-a-kind.)
3. Say, "Each one of you has a unique or one-of-a-kind body."
4. Say that we are going to prove it by comparing family member's body parts. Using the magnifying glass compare these parts:

   hair   toes
   noses   fingernails
   eyes   ear lobes
   eyelashes   freckles

5. Everyone takes turns saying this cheer:
   I'm _____ _____
              (first)   (last name)
        Couldn't be prouder.
        If you can't hear me
        I'll yell a little louder!
        (Repeat)
6. Read the Bible reference and thank God for something special about each family member.

32

I Have a Unique Body

MATERIALS: White typing paper
Washable paints, food coloring, or ink stamp pad
Magnifying glass (optional)
Bibles

BIBLE REFERENCE: 1 Corinthians 6:19, 20

FAMILY CELEBRATION
1. Ask, "What did we talk about in the last celebration?"
2. Ask, "Why do detectives look for fingerprints when they are solving a mystery?"
3. Say, "No one in the world has fingerprints, footprints, and mouth prints that are exactly like another person's prints."
4. Prove that each person's prints are indeed unique. Each person makes a design on his paper by dipping each fingertip in paint or ink pad, then presses the fingertip on his paper. Use all ten fingers. Change colors as you wish. (Optional: Make different animals by adding head, tail, legs, etc. to the fingerprint bodies.) If there is

interest, add full handprints, part or entire footprint and mouth prints. (Use lipstick for lip prints.)

5. Examine each other's prints (use magnifying glass for a detailed look). Ask, "Are each person's prints unique?"

6. Read the Bible reference and talk about what the verse says about our bodies.

7. Sing "I Am Special" (tune of "Are You Sleeping?")

> I am special!
> I am special!
> If you look, you will see:
> All are very special.
> I am very special!
> Yes, It's Me!
> Yes, It's Me!

Optional: Children might like to collect fingerprints of friends, along with their autographs. They can talk about their collections during a family celebration time.

8. Closing prayer: Lord, You made us amazingly different from each other. Thank You that I'm not a product of an assembly line, but a special creation of a God so caring about me that even my fingerprints are unlike any other. We praise You, Lord! Amen.

33

I Thank God for My Unique Body

MATERIALS: Story, "You Look Ridiculous"
Toothpicks
Small and large-sized marshmallows (optional: small colored gumdrops)
Glue (In small bowl of electric mixer, beat 1½ cups confectioners' sugar and 1 egg white. Beat until mixture is thick enough to hold a definite shape.)

FAMILY CELEBRATION
1. Read the story, "You Look Ridiculous."
2. Each family member makes one of the animals using the marshmallows, gumdrops, and toothpicks.
3. Place Hilda in the center of the table and reenact the story using the marshmallow animals.
4. Ask, "What did Hilda realize at the end of the story?"
5. Ask, "What message does this story have for us?"
6. Read Jeremiah 1:5 and talk about its meaning to you.

The Ridiculous, Happy Hippo

Hilda was a darling hippopotamus. Her favorite place to relax in the whole jungle was a large mud puddle.

One day, as she was taking a mud bath, Morris Monkey swung down from his tree to talk to her.

"Hilda, you look ridiculous," said the monkey.

"I do?" replied Hilda. "Why?"

"Because you don't have a long tail," replied the monkey. "Everyone should have a long tail to help him swing from tree to tree," added Morris.

"Dear me," said Hilda, "I have never thought about that!"

Before long, Emma Elephant sauntered along.

"What a shame," sneered Emma, "that you don't have ears like mine. You certainly look ridiculous with those small ears. Large ears make an animal look so important."

Emma walked away proudly flapping her huge ears, and Hilda felt very sad.

Travis Turtle was Hilda's next visitor. He slowly made his way to the edge of Hilda's pond. "Hilda," he said, "why don't you have a shell like mine? You look absolutely ridiculous without a shell. You can't protect yourself from enemies without one, you know."

Now Hilda began to cry. She had never felt sadder in her whole life. Soon she was so tired that she lay down to sleep. As she slept, she began to dream. In her dream, she pictured herself with the tail of a monkey, the ears of an elephant, and the shell of a turtle. She ran through the jungle shouting, "Look, look, I don't look ridiculous anymore." All the animals began to laugh. Hilda kept running until she came to her puddle. She looked into it. What she saw shocked her so much that she woke right up.

Hilda was so happy when she realized that she was just herself with no extra parts that she exclaimed, "I'm so glad that I am nobody else, just fat happy Hilda Hippo!"

34

I Have a Unique Personality

MATERIALS: Bibles or Bible storybook with story of Jacob and Esau
Pencils

BIBLE REFERENCE: Genesis 25:19-34; Genesis 27:1-45

FAMILY CELEBRATION
1. Say, "I am going to read a Bible story about two boys named Jacob and Esau. Listen for details describing each boy."
2. Read the story.
3. Ask, "How did each boy look? What else do you know about Jacob? About Esau?" (likes, dislikes, actions, how they treat other people, etc.)
4. Say, "We have just described the unique personalities of twins. Now we are going to play a game that will show us how each family member has a unique personality."
5. Read the topics below. Each family member says the first idea that pops into his head.
    (example: happiness—*skateboard, puppy,* etc.)
    United States, happiness, TV program, friend, food, Saturday, game
6. Closing prayer: Thank You, God, that I don't have to copy someone else's personality. I'm glad that the one You gave me is just right for me. Amen.

35

I Have Unique
Likes and Dislikes

MATERIALS: Bible
Activity sheet 17
Pens or pencils (one for each family member)

BIBLE REFERENCE: Psalm 139:1-12

FAMILY CELEBRATION
1. Fill in the answers on the opinion poll. (Younger children will need to have an adult write their answers for them.)
2. Compare your answers. Ask, "Do you think the other family members are silly because they did not write the same answers you did?" Discuss the fact that our different likes and dislikes are part of what makes us unique. Ask, "What do you think the world would be like if everyone liked the same kind of clothes, the same style of house, the same job, etc.?"
3. Read the Bible reference. Thank God for making a world of variety, even to the things that we like and dislike.

36

I Have Unique Feelings

MATERIALS: Bibles

Activity sheet 18

Pencils

BIBLE REFERENCE: Mark 14:32-42

FAMILY CELEBRATION
1. Say, "Jesus had feelings just like we do. Listen to the following story about Jesus, and be ready to answer the question: *What do you think Jesus' feelings were in this story?"*
2. Read the story and talk about the above question.
3. Do activity sheet 18.
4. Each family member "shows 'n tells" his activity page.
5. Ask, "Did everyone have all the same happenings and feelings?" "Does each one of us have unique feelings?"
6. Say together the following statement:

> I'm one-of-a-kind.
> Though you look the whole world over
> You will not find
> Another me.
> I'm one-of-a-kind!

Note: Children may enjoy drawing their own "feeling" cartoon faces. This activity could be used during the celebration time or before the next celebration time.

37

I Can Talk About My Feelings

MATERIALS: Bibles
Balloon
Baking soda
Vinegar
Empty pop bottle
Song, "If You're Happy" (page 175)

BIBLE REFERENCE: Ephesians 4:26, 27

FAMILY CELEBRATION
1. Say, "We are going to do an experiment and then talk about what we learned from the experiment."
2. Give the children the following instructions: Put 2 teaspoons of baking soda into the balloon. Pour 1 inch of vinegar into the bottle. Fit the neck of the balloon onto the neck of the bottle, allowing the baking soda to fall into the vinegar. Watch what happens. (The chemical action will cause the air to expand and make the balloon enlarge.)
3. Read the Bible reference, then answer together these questions: What advice does this verse give to us? Is it good advice? Why? (What happened to the balloon when the forced air could not escape?) What happens to us when we keep our anger inside? How can we get rid of our anger without being destructive?
4. Sing together, "If You're Happy," using variation. Ask, "Would anyone like to tell us about something that makes him feel angry or sad?" Take your problems to the Lord in prayer.

38

I Have a Unique Imagination

MATERIALS: Bibles
Activity sheet 19 (on back of 8)
Felt-tip pens or crayons

BIBLE REFERENCE: Psalm 8:3-9

FAMILY CELEBRATION
1. Say, "Can anyone remember what we talked about in our last celebration?" (unique feelings) "Today, we are going to prove that each of us has a unique imagination."
2. Using activity sheet 19, each family member makes four (4) "unique" pictures using the given lines.
3. Each family member "shows 'n tells" his pictures.
4. Ask, "Is each person's picture unique (one-of-a-kind)?" "Did we prove that each one of us has a 'unique' imagination?"
5. Read Psalm 8:3-9. Sing a favorite song of praise.

39

I Have Unique Abilities

MATERIALS: Bibles
Poster board or heavy paper
Felt-tip pens
Glue
Masking tape

BIBLE REFERENCE: Ephesians 4:7

FAMILY CELEBRATION
1. Read the reference and ask, "What does this verse say about each one of us?"
2. Each family member tells one special ability that each of the other family members possess.
3. Each family member makes a talent badge for the person on his left. Cut a circle from poster board. Write the name of a special ability on the circle. Attach a ribbon to the bottom of the circle. Roll masking tape into a circle and apply to the back of the badge.
4. Each person presents the badge he has made to the other member of the family.
5. Thank You, God, for giving each one of us some special abilities. Help us to use our abilities to make the world a happier place.

40

I Can Celebrate My Uniqueness

MATERIALS: Ice cream, nuts, toppings, marshmallows, chocolate chips, cherries, etc.
Bowls and spoons

BIBLE REFERENCE: Genesis 1:26, 27, 31; Matthew 22:37-39

FAMILY CELEBRATION
1. Read the Bible references.
2. Ask, "What do these verses say about you?"
3. Ask, "Why do we have reason to celebrate?"
4. Have a celebration. Arrange ice cream and toppings on the table. Let each family member make his own one-of-a-kind sundae. (Note that each person's sundae is one-of-a-kind just as each person is.)
5. "Dear God, You made each one of us special and unique. Thank You. Amen."

41

My Power Source

MATERIALS: Bibles

2 cups of rice (or torn paper) scattered on two separate areas of the floor

A broom and dustpan

A vacuum cleaner

BIBLE REFERENCE: Acts 16:22-35

FAMILY CELEBRATION

1. Say, "We are going to have a race between a broom and a vacuum cleaner." Choose two family members to participate in the race. One will clean up the rice with the broom and the dustpan. The other person will use the vacuum cleaner. Have the race. Ask, "Why did the vacuum cleaner win?" (It had extra power.)
2. Say, "While I read the following Bible story listen for different ways in which Paul and Silas showed extraordinary power."
3. Read the Bible reference.
4. Ask, "How did Paul and Silas show extraordinary power?" (They prayed and sang hymns in jail. They did not run away when they had the opportunity.)
5. Ask, "Where did this extraordinary power come from?"
6. Tomorrow we will discover how you can have this extraordinary power.
7. Tell about a time when God gave you extra power, then thank Him for it.

42

I Can Have Extraordinary Power

MATERIALS: Bibles
Popcorn kernels for popping
Ingredients and utensils for making popcorn
Poster board or cardboard
Glue
Juice or other drink
Activity sheet 20
(For optional activity: cardboard, glue, pencil, popcorn kernels and other seeds)

BIBLE REFERENCE: Ephesians 1:18b-20

FAMILY CELEBRATION
1. Ask, "What did we discuss in our last celebration?" (The extraordinary power of Paul and Silas.)
2. Ask, "Would you like to have this extraordinary power?"
3. Say, "I will read a Bible reference. Listen closely to find out who can have this power."
4. Read the Bible reference.
5. Ask, "Who can have this power?"

6. Give each family member some kernels of popcorn.
   Ask, "What can we add to these special seeds to make them become even more special, and fulfill their intended purpose?" (oil and heat)
7. Say, "Just like the popcorn seed, you are not all that God intended you to be (even though you are very special) until you have a powerful ingredient in your life. This ingredient is called the Holy Spirit." Read John 14:15-21. You may want to talk about how the Spirit works in the Christian's life.
8. Have a minute of silent prayer during which family members may ask God for His power in their lives.
9. Each family member may cut out a badge from the activity sheet 20. Glue onto a piece of cardboard or poster board. Tape a pin on the back and proudly wear it.
10. Pop the popcorn and celebrate.

Optional activity: Children may, today or another day, make popcorn signs:
   Draw the words "HOLY SPIRIT POWER" on the cardboard.
   Glue corn kernels over the lines.
   Glue contrasting seeds around the words to form the background.
   Display in a prominent place.

43

I Am Special!

MATERIALS: A mirror for each family member with the words "I Am Special" written on mirror with permanent marker. (The mirrors may be gift-wrapped.)
Activity sheets 21 and 22

FAMILY CELEBRATION
1. Present each person with a mirror. Ask, "Who is special?"
2. Say, "Today's celebration is the last one in this book. We have seen in this book that God made each one of us very special. Let's recall some of the ways in which each of us is special."
3. Read the instructions and complete activity sheet 21.
4. Have family members who can read to take turns reading the verses printed on activity sheet 22.
5. Display mirrors in individual bedrooms as a daily reminder that each family member is special.

Activity Sheet 1

To make this personal Bible bookplate for your Bible, fill in the blanks and cut out and tape the bookplate into your Bible. (Each sheet contains bookplates for two Bibles.)

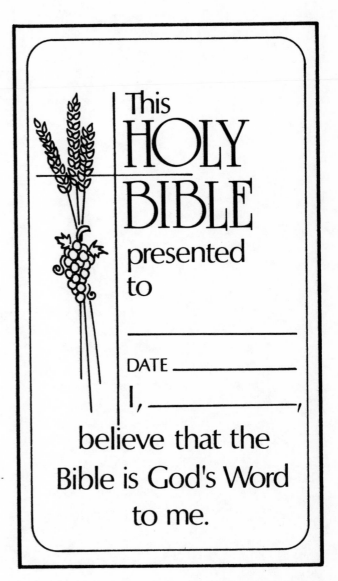

Activity Sheet 1

To make this personal Bible bookplate for your Bible, fill in the blanks and cut out and tape the bookplate into your Bible. (Each sheet contains bookplates for two Bibles.)

This
HOLY
BIBLE
presented
to

_____

DATE _____

I, _____,

believe that the
Bible is God's Word
to me.

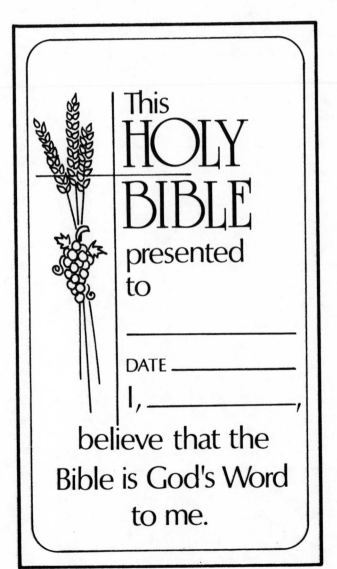

This
HOLY
BIBLE
presented
to

_____

DATE _____

I, _____,

believe that the
Bible is God's Word
to me.

Activity Sheet 2

To solve this puzzle, skip every other letter in one trip around the circle.
Print the letters on the blanks inside the Bible.

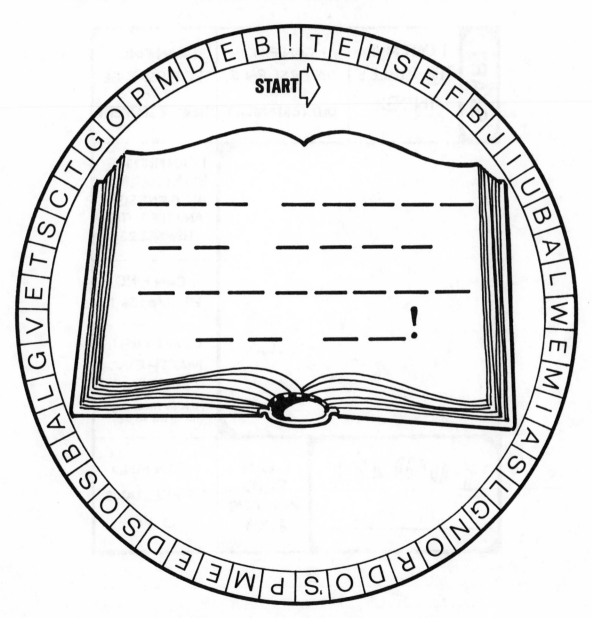

Activity Sheet 3
I CAN FIND IT

START	I CAN FIND THE BIBLE'S INDEX	I CAN FIND THE FIRST PAGE OF THE OLD TESTAMENT	I CAN FIND THE FIRST PAGE OF THE NEW TESTAMENT
			I CAN FIND THE BIG NUMBER 1 IN GENESIS AND THE LITTLE NUMBER 26.
			I CAN FIND PSALM 136:1
			I CAN FIND MATTHEW 28:20 b (b is for the second half of the verse.)
I DID IT! _____		I CAN FIND ROMANS 8:39	I CAN FIND EPHESIANS 3:17

Activity Sheet 5

CERTIFICATE OF OWNERSHIP

This is to certify that

_____

belongs to God

Child's statement of recognition:

I, _____ , believe the following statement:

"God made me and I belong to Him." (Psalm 100:3)

_____
(date)

_____
(child's signature)

_____
(parent's signature)

_____
(parent's signature)

CERTIFICATE OF OWNERSHIP

This is to certify that

_____

belongs to God

Child's statement of recognition:

I, _____ , believe the following statement:

"God made me and I belong to Him." (Psalm100:3)

_____
(date)

_____
(child's signature)

_____
(parent's signature)

_____
(parent's signature)

CERTIFICATE OF OWNERSHIP

This is to certify that

_____

belongs to God

Child's statement of recognition:

I, _____ , believe the following statement:

"God made me and I belong to Him." (Psalm 100:3)

_____
(date)

_____
(child's signature)

_____
(parent's signature)

_____
(parent's signature)

Activity Sheet 6

Psalm 119:73a

The wind separated his sailboat from Peter.

John 3:16

Peter bought his boat back
with his money.

Isaiah 59:2

Peter made his sailboat.

Activity Sheet 6

Psalm 119:73a   The wind separated his sail-
                   boat from Peter.

John 3:16   Peter bought his boat back
                   with his money.

Isaiah 59:2   Peter made his sailboat.

Activity Sheet 6

Psalm 119:73a   The wind separated his sail-
                       boat from Peter.

John 3:16   Peter bought his boat back
                       with his money.

Isaiah 59:2   Peter made his sailboat.

Activity Sheet 6

Psalm 119:73a

The wind separated his sailboat from Peter.

John 3:16

Peter bought his boat back
with his money.

Isaiah 59:2

Peter made his sailboat.

Activity Sheet 7

Decode the following messages about God's love. (Use the key at the bottom of the page.)

GOD'S CONSTANT LOVE IS A

 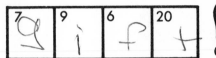

(Ephesians 2:8, 9)

NOTHING CAN

US THE

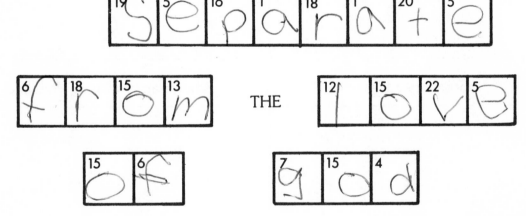

(Romans 8:37-39)

a	b	c	d	e	f	g	h	i	j	k	l	m	n	o	p	q	r	s	t	u	v	w	x	y	z
1	2	3	4	5	6	7	8	9	10	11	12	13	14	15	16	17	18	19	20	21	22	23	24	25	26

Activity Sheet 12
DAVID AND GOLIATH

The Philistines and Israelite Armies

David fighting Goliath

Goliath dead

Israelite army chasing Philistines

Activity Sheet 7

Decode the following messages about God's love. (Use the key at the bottom of the page.)

GOD'S CONSTANT LOVE IS A

6	18	5	5

7	9	6	20

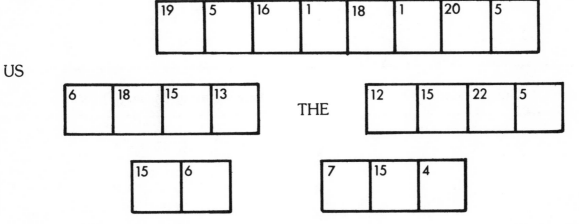

(Ephesians 2:8, 9)

NOTHING CAN

19	5	16	1	18	1	20	5

US

6	18	15	13

THE

12	15	22	5

15	6

7	15	4

(Romans 8:37-39)

a	b	c	d	e	f	g	h	i	j	k	l	m	n	o	p	q	r	s	t	u	v	w	x	y	z
1	2	3	4	5	6	7	8	9	10	11	12	13	14	15	16	17	18	19	20	21	22	23	24	25	26

Activity Sheet 12
DAVID AND GOLIATH

The Philistines and Israelite Armies

David fighting Goliath

Goliath dead

Israelite army chasing Philistines

Activity Sheet 7

Decode the following messages about God's love. (Use the key at the bottom of the page.)

GOD'S CONSTANT LOVE IS A

6	18	5	5

7	9	6	20

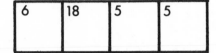

(Ephesians 2:8, 9)

NOTHING CAN

19	5	16	1	18	1	20	5

US

6	18	15	13

THE

12	15	22	5

15	6

7	15	4

(Romans 8:37-39)

a	b	c	d	e	f	g	h	i	j	k	l	m	n	o	p	q	r	s	t	u	v	w	x	y	z
1	2	3	4	5	6	7	8	9	10	11	12	13	14	15	16	17	18	19	20	21	22	23	24	25	26

Activity Sheet 12
DAVID AND GOLIATH

The Philistines and Israelite Armies

David fighting Goliath

Goliath dead

Israelite army chasing Philistines

Activity Sheet 7

Decode the following messages about God's love. (Use the key at the bottom of the page.)

GOD'S CONSTANT LOVE IS A

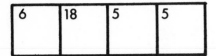

| 6 | 18 | 5 | 5 |

| 7 | 9 | 6 | 20 |

(Ephesians 2:8, 9)

NOTHING CAN

| 19 | 5 | 16 | 1 | 18 | 1 | 20 | 5 |

US

| 6 | 18 | 15 | 13 | THE | 12 | 15 | 22 | 5 |

| 15 | 6 | | 7 | 15 | 4 |

(Romans 8:37-39)

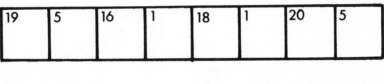

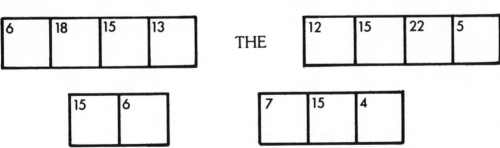

a	b	c	d	e	f	g	h	i	j	k	l	m	n	o	p	q	r	s	t	u	v	w	x	y	z
1	2	3	4	5	6	7	8	9	10	11	12	13	14	15	16	17	18	19	20	21	22	23	24	25	26

109

Activity Sheet 12
DAVID AND GOLIATH

The Philistines and Israelite Armies

David fighting Goliath

Goliath dead

Israelite army chasing Philistines

FAMILY TEAM WORK

Fill in the blanks with ways your family helps one another. (Smaller children may draw pictures.)

1. Mother helps Dad _____

2. Dad helps Mom _____

3. I (child) help Mother _____

4. I (child) help Dad _____

5. I (child) help my sister(s) _____

6. I (child) help my brother(s) _____

7. Dad helps me _____

8. Mom helps me _____

9. We all help together _____

My Family Needs Me!

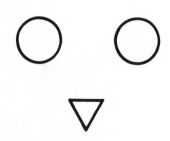

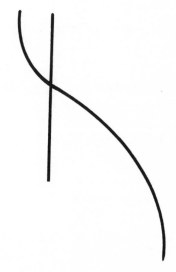

Activity Sheet 8
FAMILY TEAM WORK

Fill in the blanks with ways your family helps one another. (Smaller children may draw pictures.)

1. Mother helps Dad _____

2. Dad helps Mom _____

3. I (child) help Mother _____

4. I (child) help Dad _____

5. I (child) help my sister(s) _____

6. I (child) help my brother(s) _____

7. Dad helps me _____

8. Mom helps me _____

9. We all help together _____

My Family Needs Me!

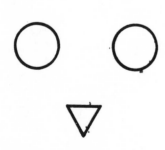

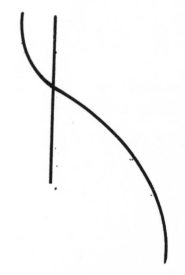

Activity Sheet 9
"AMAZING BRAIN" WORD SEARCH

Find fourteen things we can do because God gave us amazing brains: hear, speak, learn, read, see, sing, write, smell, move, taste, think, solve problems, remember, imagine. Hidden words are written down and across.

```
S  R  S  A  M  A  R  P  L  E  R  S  W  I  H
M  H  E  B  C  S  M  E  L  L  E  E  R  N  S
L  E  P  S  I  N  G  L  Q  C  M  P  I  T  R
S  A  L  K  E  O  T  S  A  D  E  E  T  O  E
O  R  M  U  H  E  R  E  M  E  M  E  E  P  A
V  Q  O  S  P  E  A  K  A  I  B  W  O  T  D
T  L  U  P  I  M  A  G  I  N  E  E  L  A  A
P  E  A  O  M  O  Q  E  A  K  R  O  S  S  R
M  A  L  R  C  V  S  E  E  O  E  H  E  T  W
O  R  E  S  H  E  P  T  H  I  N  K  R  E  T
L  N  S  O  L  V  E  P  R  O  B  L  E  M  S
```

Activity Sheet 10

There is only one way through this maze to the happy face!
Can you find it? Draw a line to the face.

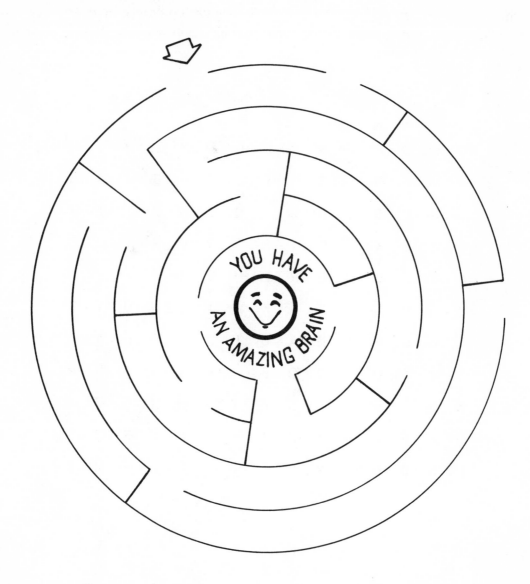

Activity Sheet 9

"AMAZING BRAIN" WORD SEARCH

Find fourteen things we can do because God gave us amazing brains: hear, speak, learn, read, see, sing, write, smell, move, taste, think, solve problems, remember, imagine. Hidden words are written down and across.

```
S R S A M A R P L E R S W I H
M H E B C S M E L L E E R N S
L E P S I N G L Q C M P I T R
S A L K E O T S A D E E T O E
O R M U H E R E M E M E E P A
V Q O S P E A K A I B W O T D
T L U P I M A G I N E E L A A
P E A O M O Q E A K R O S S R
M A L R C V S E E O E H E T W
O R E S H E P T H I N K R E T
L N S O L V E P R O B L E M S
```

Activity Sheet 10

There is only one way through this maze to the happy face!
Can you find it? Draw a line to the face.

Activity Sheet 9
"AMAZING BRAIN" WORD SEARCH

Find fourteen things we can do because God gave us amazing brains: hear, speak, learn, read, see, sing, write, smell, move, taste, think, solve problems, remember, imagine. Hidden words are written down and across.

```
S R S A M A R P L E R S W I H
M H E B C S M E L L E E R N S
L E P S I N G L Q C M P I T R
S A L K E O T S A D E E T O E
O R M U H E R E M E M E E P A
V Q O S P E A K A I B W O T D
T L U P I M A G I N E E L A A
P E A O M O Q E A K R O S S R
M A L R C V S E E O E H E T W
O R E S H E P T H I N K R E T
L N S O L V E P R O B L E M S
```

Activity Sheet 10

There is only one way through this maze to the happy face!
Can you find it? Draw a line to the face.

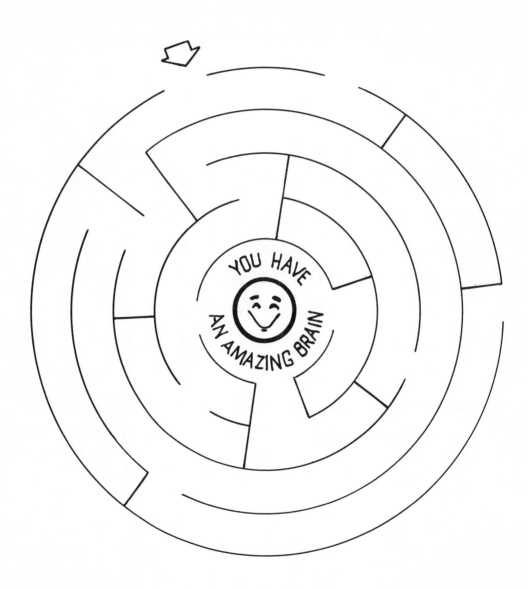

Activity Sheet 9
"AMAZING BRAIN" WORD SEARCH

Find fourteen things we can do because God gave us amazing brains: hear, speak, learn, read, see, sing, write, smell, move, taste, think, solve problems, remember, imagine. Hidden words are written down and across.

```
S R S A M A R P L E R S W I H
M H E B C S M E L L E E R N S
L E P S I N G L Q C M P I T R
S A L K E O T S A D E E T O E
O R M U H E R E M E M E E P A
V Q O S P E A K A I B W O T D
T L U P I M A G I N E E L A A
P E A O M O Q E A K R O S S R
M A L R C V S E E O E H E T W
O R E S H E P T H I N K R E T
L N S O L V E P R O B L E M S
```

Activity Sheet 10

There is only one way through this maze to the happy face!
Can you find it? Draw a line to the face.

YOU HAVE
AN AMAZING BRAIN

Activity Sheet 11

✓A friend loves at all times.   Proverbs 17:17

Be kind . . . to one another.   Ephesians 4:32

Create in me a pure heart, O God.   Psalm 51:10

Draw near to God with a sincere heart.   Hebrews 10:22

Even a child is known by his actions.   Proverbs 20:11

Fear God and keep his commandments.   Ecclesiastes 12:13

God is love.   1 John 4:8

Honor your father and your mother.   Exodus 20:12

If you love me, you will obey what I command.   John 14:15

Jesus said, "Let the little children come to me."   Matthew 19:14

Keep your tongue from evil.   Psalm 34:13

Love one another.   1 John 3:23

My son, give me your heart.   Proverbs 23:26

No one can serve two masters.   Matthew 6:24

✓ *O* Lord my God, you are very great.   Psalm 104:1

Praise the Lord.   Psalm 148:1

Quench not the Spirit.   1 Thessalonians 5:19, *KJV*

Remember the Sabbath day by keeping it holy.   Exodus 20:8

Seek the Lord while he may be found.   Isaiah 55:6

Teach me your way, O Lord.   Psalm 27:11

Under his wings you will find refuge.   Psalm 91:4

Verily there is a reward for the righteous.   Psalm 58:11, *KJV*

When I am afraid, I will trust in you.   Psalm 56:3

X Exalt the Lord our God.   Psalm 99:5

You are the light of the world.   Matthew 5:14

Zion hears and rejoices.   Psalm 97:8

Activity Sheet 11

A friend loves at all times.	Proverbs 17:17
Be kind . . . to one another.	Ephesians 4:32
*C*reate in me a pure heart, O God.	Psalm 51:10
*D*raw near to God with a sincere heart.	Hebrews 10:22
*E*ven a child is known by his actions.	Proverbs 20:11
*F*ear God and keep his commandments.	Ecclesiastes 12:13
*G*od is love.	1 John 4:8
*H*onor your father and your mother.	Exodus 20:12
*I*f you love me, you will obey what I command.	John 14:15
*J*esus said, "Let the little children come to me."	Matthew 19:14
*K*eep your tongue from evil.	Psalm 34:13
*L*ove one another.	1 John 3:23
*M*y son, give me your heart.	Proverbs 23:26
*N*o one can serve two masters.	Matthew 6:24
O Lord my God, you are very great.	Psalm 104:1
*P*raise the Lord.	Psalm 148:1
*Q*uench not the Spirit.	1 Thessalonians 5:19, *KJV*
*R*emember the Sabbath day by keeping it holy.	Exodus 20:8
*S*eek the Lord while he may be found.	Isaiah 55:6
*T*each me your way, O Lord.	Psalm 27:11
*U*nder his wings you will find refuge.	Psalm 91:4
*V*erily there is a reward for the righteous.	Psalm 58:11, *KJV*
*W*hen I am afraid, I will trust in you.	Psalm 56:3
X Exalt the Lord our God.	Psalm 99:5
*Y*ou are the light of the world.	Matthew 5:14
*Z*ion hears and rejoices.	Psalm 97:8

Activity Sheet 11

A friend loves at all times.	Proverbs 17:17
Be kind . . . to one another.	Ephesians 4:32
Create in me a pure heart, O God.	Psalm 51:10
Draw near to God with a sincere heart.	Hebrews 10:22
Even a child is known by his actions.	Proverbs 20:11
Fear God and keep his commandments.	Ecclesiastes 12:13
God is love.	1 John 4:8
Honor your father and your mother.	Exodus 20:12
If you love me, you will obey what I command.	John 14:15
Jesus said, "Let the little children come to me."	Matthew 19:14
Keep your tongue from evil.	Psalm 34:13
Love one another.	1 John 3:23
My son, give me your heart.	Proverbs 23:26
No one can serve two masters.	Matthew 6:24
O Lord my God, you are very great.	Psalm 104:1
Praise the Lord.	Psalm 148:1
Quench not the Spirit.	1 Thessalonians 5:19, *KJV*
Remember the Sabbath day by keeping it holy.	Exodus 20:8
Seek the Lord while he may be found.	Isaiah 55:6
Teach me your way, O Lord.	Psalm 27:11
Under his wings you will find refuge.	Psalm 91:4
Verily there is a reward for the righteous.	Psalm 58:11, *KJV*
When I am afraid, I will trust in you.	Psalm 56:3
X Exalt the Lord our God.	Psalm 99:5
You are the light of the world.	Matthew 5:14
Zion hears and rejoices.	Psalm 97:8

Activity Sheet 11

A friend loves at all times.

Be kind . . . to one another.

Create in me a pure heart, O God.

Draw near to God with a sincere heart.

Even a child is known by his actions.

Fear God and keep his commandments.

God is love.

Honor your father and your mother.

If you love me, you will obey what I command.

Jesus said, "Let the little children come to me."

Keep your tongue from evil.

Love one another.

My son, give me your heart.

No one can serve two masters.

O Lord my God, you are very great.

Praise the Lord.

Quench not the Spirit.

Remember the Sabbath day by keeping it holy.

Seek the Lord while he may be found.

Teach me your way, O Lord.

Under his wings you will find refuge.

Verily there is a reward for the righteous.

When I am afraid, I will trust in you.

X Exalt the Lord our God.

You are the light of the world.

Zion hears and rejoices.

Proverbs 17:17

Ephesians 4:32

Psalm 51:10

Hebrews 10:22

Proverbs 20:11

Ecclesiastes 12:13

1 John 4:8

Exodus 20:12

John 14:15

Matthew 19:14

Psalm 34:13

1 John 3:23

Proverbs 23:26

Matthew 6:24

Psalm 104:1

Psalm 148:1

1 Thessalonians 5:19, *KJV*

Exodus 20:8

Isaiah 55:6

Psalm 27:11

Psalm 91:4

Psalm 58:11, *KJV*

Psalm 56:3

Psalm 99:5

Matthew 5:14

Psalm 97:8

Activity Sheet 13
I CAN CHOOSE

(This page is for children and teenagers. Adults use the next page.)

STEP 1   Ask yourself, "What are the possible choices?"
Write your choice on the line.
1. I am late for a party. Walking down the sidewalk I notice a girl who has fallen off her bike and hurt herself. She is crying. I

   would _____.

2. I am playing baseball. Suddenly the ball goes through the neighbor's

   garage window. I feel like running home. I would _____

   _____.

3. A new boy (or girl) comes to our school. All the children are playing together in groups. The new child is all by himself. I

   would _____.

4. I am at the store. I see a friend. He puts a ring into his pocket and says, "Go ahead and take one. No one will ever know." I

   would _____.

STEP 2   Share your choices with the rest of the family.

STEP 3   Rate your choices: Was my choice a G.C. (GOOD CHOICE) or a B.C. (BAD CHOICE)? Consider this: Did my choice show love for God, others, and self? Now write B.C. or G.C. beside each choice.

STEP 4   Closing: Everyone pray together: "Help me, God, to make good choices. Help me always to show love to You, others, and myself. Amen."

Activity Sheet 15

I CAN GROW MENTALLY

	DO A CROSSWORD PUZZLE
	MULTIPLY
	DIVIDE
	SEW ON A BUTTON
	USE A DICTIONARY
	IDENTIFY 10 BIRDS
	IDENTIFY 5 TREES
	NAME THE PRESIDENT AND VICE PRESIDENT
	SAY THE "LORD'S PRAYER"
	NAME AND LOCATE 25 STATES
	ADD 2-DIGIT NUMBERS
	SUBTRACT 2-DIGIT NUMBERS
	TELL 5 IMPORTANT FACTS ABOUT MY STATE
	FIND BIBLE REFERENCES
	PLAY 5 GAMES (Life, Checkers, etc.)
	PLAY A SONG ON A MUSICAL INSTRUMENT
	BUILD SOMETHING
	BAKE SOMETHING
	WRITE A POEM
	DRAW A PICTURE
	SAY THE "PLEDGE OF ALLEGIANCE"
	MEMORIZE A POEM
	MEMORIZE 3 BIBLE VERSES
	COUNT TO 10
	SPELL MY NAME
	SAY MY PHONE NUMBER
	SAY MY ADDRESS
	READ A SENTENCE
	TIE MY SHOELACES
	WALK BY MYSELF
	FEED MYSELF

Activity Sheet 13
I CAN CHOOSE

(This page is for children and teenagers. Adults use the next page.)

STEP 1   Ask yourself, "What are the possible choices?"
Write your choice on the line.
1. I am late for a party. Walking down the sidewalk I notice a girl who has fallen off her bike and hurt herself. She is crying. I

   would _____.

2. I am playing baseball. Suddenly the ball goes through the neighbor's

   garage window. I feel like running home. I would _____

   _____.

3. A new boy (or girl) comes to our school. All the children are playing together in groups. The new child is all by himself. I

   would _____.

4. I am at the store. I see a friend. He puts a ring into his pocket and says, "Go ahead and take one. No one will ever know." I

   would _____.

STEP 2   Share your choices with the rest of the family.

STEP 3   Rate your choices: Was my choice a G.C. (GOOD CHOICE) or a B.C. (BAD CHOICE)? Consider this: Did my choice show love for God, others, and self? Now write B.C. or G.C. beside each choice.

STEP 4   Closing: Everyone pray together: "Help me, God, to make good choices. Help me always to show love to You, others, and myself. Amen."

Activity Sheet 15

I CAN GROW MENTALLY

	DO A CROSSWORD PUZZLE
	MULTIPLY
	DIVIDE
	SEW ON A BUTTON
	USE A DICTIONARY
	IDENTIFY 10 BIRDS
	IDENTIFY 5 TREES
	NAME THE PRESIDENT AND VICE PRESIDENT
	SAY THE "LORD'S PRAYER"
	NAME AND LOCATE 25 STATES
	ADD 2-DIGIT NUMBERS
	SUBTRACT 2-DIGIT NUMBERS
	TELL 5 IMPORTANT FACTS ABOUT MY STATE
	FIND BIBLE REFERENCES
	PLAY 5 GAMES (Life, Checkers, etc.)
	PLAY A SONG ON A MUSICAL INSTRUMENT
	BUILD SOMETHING
	BAKE SOMETHING
	WRITE A POEM
	DRAW A PICTURE
	SAY THE "PLEDGE OF ALLEGIANCE"
	MEMORIZE A POEM
	MEMORIZE 3 BIBLE VERSES
	COUNT TO 10
	SPELL MY NAME
	SAY MY PHONE NUMBER
	SAY MY ADDRESS
	READ A SENTENCE
	TIE MY SHOELACES
	WALK BY MYSELF
	FEED MYSELF

Activity Sheet 14
I CAN CHOOSE

(This page is for adults.)

STEP 1   Think about the statements below. Ask yourself
1. What are the possible choices?
2. What would I choose?
3. Write a short answer.

1. I am late for a party. As I drive out of my driveway, I notice a girl who has fallen off her bike and hurt herself. I would _____
_____.

2. I have borrowed a suitcase from my friend. When I return from my trip I notice that the handle is broken. I decide that if I don't say anything my friend will think it was like that before I borrowed it. I would _____.

3. I am making a guest list for a party with good friends. A new family has just moved into my neighborhood. I would _____
_____.

4. I have just returned home after shopping and discover that the clerk made a mistake when she gave me a refund. She gave me $5.00 too much. I would _____.

STEP 2   Share your choices with the rest of the family.

STEP 3   Rate your choices: Was my choice a G.C. (GOOD CHOICE) or a B.C. (BAD CHOICE)? Consider this: Did my choice show love for God, others, and self? Write B.C. or G.C. beside each choice.

STEP 4   Closing: Everyone pray together: "Help me, God, to make good choices. Help me always to show love to You, others, and myself. Amen."

Activity Sheet 15

I CAN GROW MENTALLY

	DO A CROSSWORD PUZZLE
	MULTIPLY
	DIVIDE
	SEW ON A BUTTON
	USE A DICTIONARY
	IDENTIFY 10 BIRDS
	IDENTIFY 5 TREES
	NAME THE PRESIDENT AND VICE PRESIDENT
	SAY THE "LORD'S PRAYER"
	NAME AND LOCATE 25 STATES
	ADD 2-DIGIT NUMBERS
	SUBTRACT 2-DIGIT NUMBERS
	TELL 5 IMPORTANT FACTS ABOUT MY STATE
	FIND BIBLE REFERENCES
	PLAY 5 GAMES (Life, Checkers, etc.)
	PLAY A SONG ON A MUSICAL INSTRUMENT
	BUILD SOMETHING
	BAKE SOMETHING
	WRITE A POEM
	DRAW A PICTURE
	SAY THE "PLEDGE OF ALLEGIANCE"
	MEMORIZE A POEM
	MEMORIZE 3 BIBLE VERSES
	COUNT TO 10
	SPELL MY NAME
	SAY MY PHONE NUMBER
	SAY MY ADDRESS
	READ A SENTENCE
	TIE MY SHOELACES
	WALK BY MYSELF
	FEED MYSELF

Activity Sheet 14
I CAN CHOOSE

(This page is for adults.)

STEP 1   Think about the statements below. Ask yourself
1. What are the possible choices?
2. What would I choose?
3. Write a short answer.

1. I am late for a party. As I drive out of my driveway, I notice a girl who has fallen off her bike and hurt herself. I would _____
    _____.

2. I have borrowed a suitcase from my friend. When I return from my trip I notice that the handle is broken. I decide that if I don't say anything my friend will think it was like that before I borrowed it. I would _____.

3. I am making a guest list for a party with good friends. A new family has just moved into my neighborhood. I would _____
    _____.

4. I have just returned home after shopping and discover that the clerk made a mistake when she gave me a refund. She gave me $5.00 too much. I would _____.

STEP 2   Share your choices with the rest of the family.

STEP 3   Rate your choices: Was my choice a G.C. (GOOD CHOICE) or a B.C. (BAD CHOICE)? Consider this: Did my choice show love for God, others, and self? Write B.C. or G.C. beside each choice.

STEP 4   Closing: Everyone pray together: "Help me, God, to make good choices. Help me always to show love to You, others, and myself. Amen."

Activity Sheet 15

I CAN GROW MENTALLY

	DO A CROSSWORD PUZZLE
	MULTIPLY
	DIVIDE
	SEW ON A BUTTON
	USE A DICTIONARY
	IDENTIFY 10 BIRDS
	IDENTIFY 5 TREES
	NAME THE PRESIDENT AND VICE PRESIDENT
	SAY THE "LORD'S PRAYER"
	NAME AND LOCATE 25 STATES
	ADD 2-DIGIT NUMBERS
	SUBTRACT 2-DIGIT NUMBERS
	TELL 5 IMPORTANT FACTS ABOUT MY STATE
	FIND BIBLE REFERENCES
	PLAY 5 GAMES (Life, Checkers, etc.)
	PLAY A SONG ON A MUSICAL INSTRUMENT
	BUILD SOMETHING
	BAKE SOMETHING
	WRITE A POEM
	DRAW A PICTURE
	SAY THE "PLEDGE OF ALLEGIANCE"
	MEMORIZE A POEM
	MEMORIZE 3 BIBLE VERSES
	COUNT TO 10
	SPELL MY NAME
	SAY MY PHONE NUMBER
	SAY MY ADDRESS
	READ A SENTENCE
	TIE MY SHOELACES
	WALK BY MYSELF
	FEED MYSELF

Activity Sheet 16

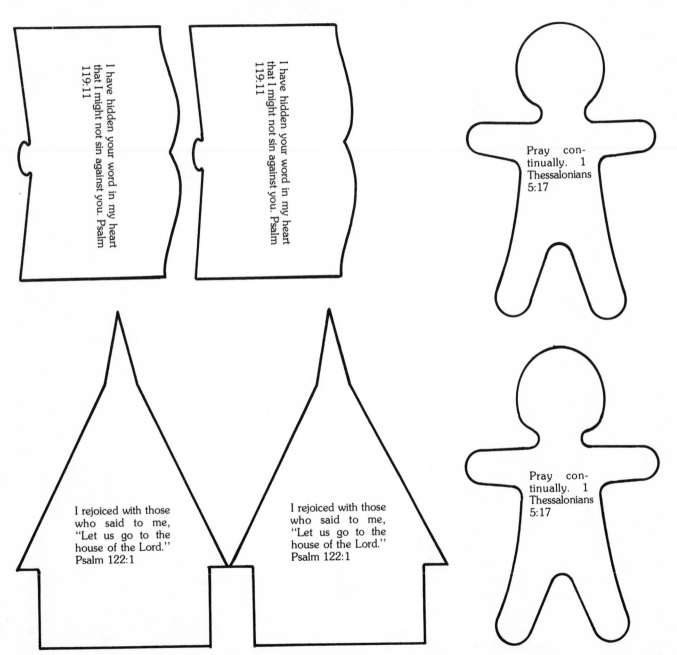

I have hidden your word in my heart that I might not sin against you. Psalm 119:11

I have hidden your word in my heart that I might not sin against you. Psalm 119:11

Pray continually. 1 Thessalonians 5:17

Pray continually. 1 Thessalonians 5:17

I rejoiced with those who said to me, "Let us go to the house of the Lord." Psalm 122:1

I rejoiced with those who said to me, "Let us go to the house of the Lord." Psalm 122:1

143

Activity Sheet 16

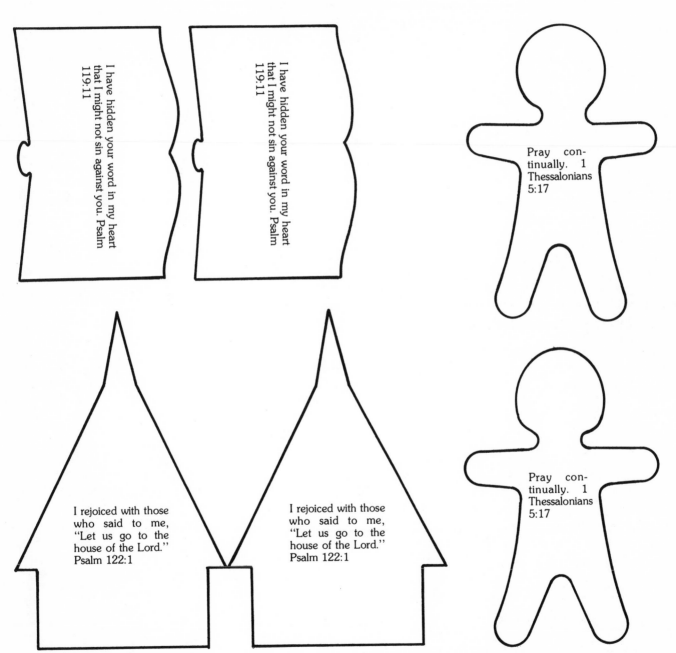

I have hidden your word in my heart that I might not sin against you. Psalm 119:11

I have hidden your word in my heart that I might not sin against you. Psalm 119:11

Pray continually. 1 Thessalonians 5:17

I rejoiced with those who said to me, "Let us go to the house of the Lord." Psalm 122:1

I rejoiced with those who said to me, "Let us go to the house of the Lord." Psalm 122:1

Pray continually. 1 Thessalonians 5:17

Activity Sheet 16

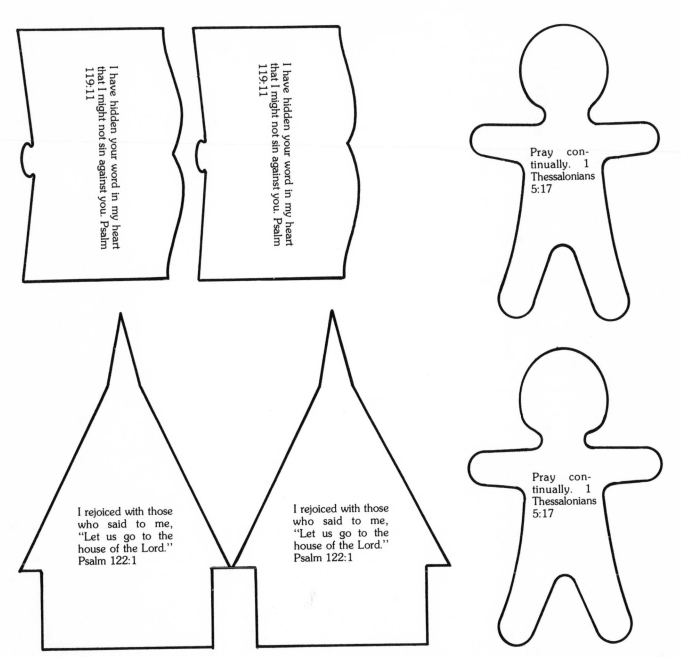

I have hidden your word in my heart that I might not sin against you. Psalm 119:11

I have hidden your word in my heart that I might not sin against you. Psalm 119:11

Pray con-
tinually. 1
Thessalonians
5:17

I rejoiced with those who said to me, "Let us go to the house of the Lord." Psalm 122:1

I rejoiced with those who said to me, "Let us go to the house of the Lord." Psalm 122:1

Pray con-
tinually. 1
Thessalonians
5:17

147

Activity Sheet 21
CHECK-UP TIME

God made you a special person. Prove again that you are special by underlining the best choices in Column B.

Column A	*Column B*
The Bible is	lots of words that are hard to understand God talking to people who lived a long time ago God's messages to me
God loves me	all the time if I don't do anything wrong when I read the Bible
Mom and Dad love me	when I get good grades when I do what they tell me to do all the time
God gave me	a body a stupid-looking body a wonderful, fantastic body
God gave me an "amazing brain"; therefore,	I don't need to study I can remember, imagine, learn, and feel anything that I think or feel is "good."
I can grow	bigger and stronger each day closer to God each day mentally (smarter) each day physically, mentally, and spiritually each day
I am unique. That means	I am better than anyone else I have a bad disease I have a "one-of-a-kind" body and personality
I thank God for	designing and making me "special" always loving me for promising to be with me and to help me at all times all of the above

Activity Sheet 22

A FAMILY RECITATION FOR CELEBRATION

Ephesians 3:14-21

14, 15   I kneel before the Father, from whom his whole family in heaven and on earth derives its name.

16   I pray that out of his glorious riches he may strengthen you with power through his Spirit in your inner being,

17, 18   so that Christ may dwell in your hearts through faith.
And I pray that you, being rooted and established in love, may have power, together with all the saints, to grasp how wide and long and high and deep is the love of Christ,

19   and to know this love that surpasses knowledge—that you may be filled to the measure of all the fullness of God.

20   Now to him who is able to do immeasurably more than all we ask or imagine, according to his power that is at work within us,

21   to him be glory in the church and in Christ Jesus throughout all generations, for ever and ever! Amen.

Activity Sheet 21
CHECK-UP TIME

God made you a special person. Prove again that you are special by underlining the best choices in Column B.

Column A	*Column B*
The Bible is	lots of words that are hard to understand God talking to people who lived a long time ago God's messages to me
God loves me	all the time if I don't do anything wrong when I read the Bible
Mom and Dad love me	when I get good grades when I do what they tell me to do all the time
God gave me	a body a stupid-looking body a wonderful, fantastic body
God gave me an "amazing brain"; therefore,	I don't need to study I can remember, imagine, learn, and feel anything that I think or feel is "good."
I can grow	bigger and stronger each day closer to God each day mentally (smarter) each day physically, mentally, and spiritually each day
I am unique. That means	I am better than anyone else I have a bad disease I have a "one-of-a-kind" body and personality
I thank God for	designing and making me "special" always loving me for promising to be with me and to help me at all times all of the above

Activity Sheet 22

A FAMILY RECITATION FOR CELEBRATION

Ephesians 3:14-21

14, 15 I kneel before the Father, from whom his whole family in heaven and on earth derives its name.

16 I pray that out of his glorious riches he may strengthen you with power through his Spirit in your inner being,

17, 18 so that Christ may dwell in your hearts through faith.
And I pray that you, being rooted and established in love, may have power, together with all the saints, to grasp how wide and long and high and deep is the love of Christ,

19 and to know this love that surpasses knowledge—that you may be filled to the measure of all the fullness of God.

20 Now to him who is able to do immeasurably more than all we ask or imagine, according to his power that is at work within us,

21 to him be glory in the church and in Christ Jesus throughout all generations, for ever and ever! Amen.

Activity Sheet 21
CHECK-UP TIME

God made you a special person. Prove again that you are special by underlining the best choices in Column B.

Column A	*Column B*
The Bible is	lots of words that are hard to understand God talking to people who lived a long time ago God's messages to me
God loves me	all the time if I don't do anything wrong when I read the Bible
Mom and Dad love me	when I get good grades when I do what they tell me to do all the time
God gave me	a body a stupid-looking body a wonderful, fantastic body
God gave me an "amazing brain"; therefore,	I don't need to study I can remember, imagine, learn, and feel anything that I think or feel is "good."
I can grow	bigger and stronger each day closer to God each day mentally (smarter) each day physically, mentally, and spiritually each day
I am unique. That means	I am better than anyone else I have a bad disease I have a "one-of-a-kind" body and personality
I thank God for	designing and making me "special" always loving me for promising to be with me and to help me at all times all of the above

Activity Sheet 22

A FAMILY RECITATION FOR CELEBRATION

Ephesians 3:14-21

14, 15   I kneel before the Father, from whom his whole family in heaven and on earth derives its name.

16   I pray that out of his glorious riches he may strengthen you with power through his Spirit in your inner being,

17, 18   so that Christ may dwell in your hearts through faith.
And I pray that you, being rooted and established in love, may have power, together with all the saints, to grasp how wide and long and high and deep is the love of Christ,

19   and to know this love that surpasses knowledge—that you may be filled to the measure of all the fullness of God.

20   Now to him who is able to do immeasurably more than all we ask or imagine, according to his power that is at work within us,

21   to him be glory in the church and in Christ Jesus throughout all generations, for ever and ever! Amen.

Activity Sheet 21
CHECK-UP TIME

God made you a special person. Prove again that you are special by underlining the best choices in Column B.

Column A	*Column B*
The Bible is	lots of words that are hard to understand
	God talking to people who lived a long time ago
	God's messages to me
God loves me	all the time
	if I don't do anything wrong
	when I read the Bible
Mom and Dad love me	when I get good grades
	when I do what they tell me to do
	all the time
God gave me	a body
	a stupid-looking body
	a wonderful, fantastic body
God gave me an "amazing brain"; therefore,	I don't need to study
	I can remember, imagine, learn, and feel
	anything that I think or feel is "good."
I can grow	bigger and stronger each day
	closer to God each day
	mentally (smarter) each day
	physically, mentally, and spiritually each day
I am unique. That means	I am better than anyone else
	I have a bad disease
	I have a "one-of-a-kind" body and personality
I thank God for	designing and making me "special"
	always loving me
	for promising to be with me and to help me at all times
	all of the above

165

Activity Sheet 22

A FAMILY RECITATION FOR CELEBRATION

Ephesians 3:14-21

14, 15   I kneel before the Father, from whom his whole family in heaven and on earth derives its name.

16   I pray that out of his glorious riches he may strengthen you with power through his Spirit in your inner being,

17, 18   so that Christ may dwell in your hearts through faith.
And I pray that you, being rooted and established in love, may have power, together with all the saints, to grasp how wide and long and high and deep is the love of Christ,

19   and to know this love that surpasses knowledge—that you may be filled to the measure of all the fullness of God.

20   Now to him who is able to do immeasurably more than all we ask or imagine, according to his power that is at work within us,

21   to him be glory in the church and in Christ Jesus throughout all generations, for ever and ever! Amen.

The B-I-B-L-E

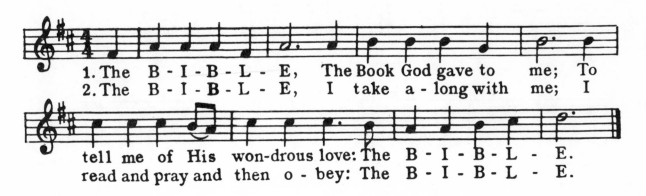

1. The B - I - B - L - E, The Book God gave to me; To
2. The B - I - B - L - E, I take a - long with me; I

tell me of His won-drous love: The B - I - B - L - E.
read and pray and then o - bey: The B - I - B - L - E.

Jesus Loves Me

Anna B. Warner, Alt.

William B. Bradbury

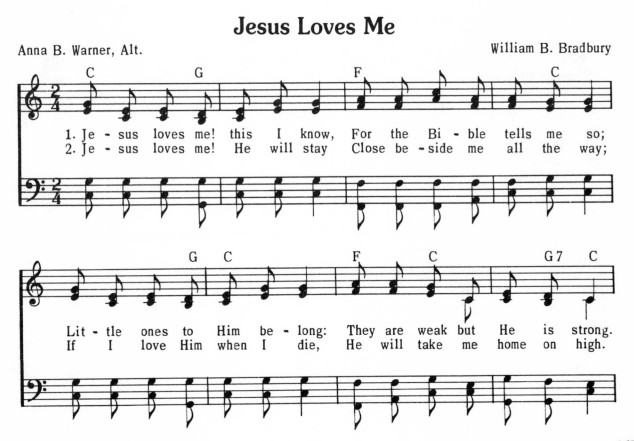

1. Je - sus loves me! this I know, For the Bi - ble tells me so;
2. Je - sus loves me! He will stay Close be - side me all the way;

Lit - tle ones to Him be - long: They are weak but He is strong.
If I love Him when I die, He will take me home on high.

CHORUS

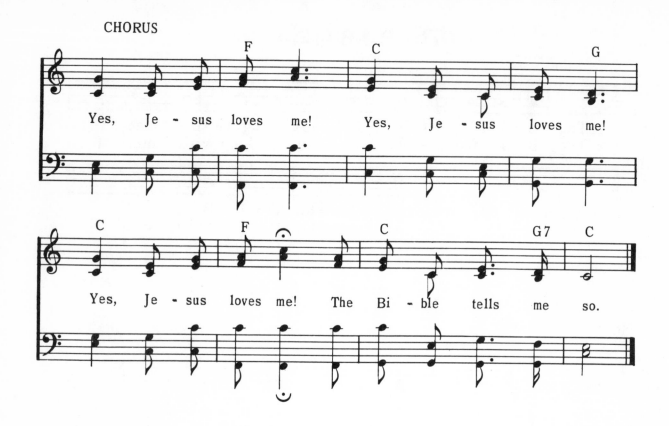

Yes, Je - sus loves me! Yes, Je - sus loves me!

Yes, Je - sus loves me! The Bi - ble tells me so.

You're Something Special

Words by William J. & Gloria Gaither

Music by William J. Gaither
Arr. by Donna Huff

1. When Je - sus sent you to us, we loved you from the start: You were
have a lit - tle sis - ter who's not at all like me: She can
dad - dy mows the back - yard, my mom - my makes the bed; My ___

just a bit of sun - shine from heav - en to our hearts. Not
write a love - ly poem ___ but I can climb a tree. My
bro - ther cleans his play - room, I see the dog gets fed. And

just an-oth-er ba-by___ 'cause since the world be-gan, There's been
bro- ther too is dif-f'rent with freck- les on his nose, When my
each one needs the oth-er___ to help him thro' the day, ___ And

some-thing ver-y spec-ial for you in His plan. That's why
ques- tions need___ an-swers, he's the one who knows. That's why
love must be the rea-son God planned it that way. That's why

CHORUS

He made you spec-ial, you're the on - ly one of your kind, God
I'm some-thing spec-ial, I'm the on - ly one of my kind, God
He made me spec-ial, I'm the on - ly one of my kind, God

170

gave you a bod-y and a bright health - y mind; He
gave me a bod-y and a bright health - y mind; He
gave me a bod-y and a bright health - y mind; He

had a spec-ial pur-pose that He want-ed you to find, so He
had a spec-ial pur-pose that He want-ed me to find, so He
had a spec-ial pur-pose that He want-ed me to find, so He

made you some-thing spec-ial, you're the on - ly one of your
made me some-thing spec-ial, I'm the on - ly one of my
made me some-thing spec-ial, I'm the on - ly one of my

The Twelve Apostles

Dana Eynon

John Leinbaugh

Je - sus called twelve men: Pe-ter, James, and John, An-drew, Thom-as, Phil- ip, too, Mat - thew, James the less, Al - so Thad - de - us, Si - mon and Bar - thol - o - mew. There was one more man— Ju - das

was his name, Who turned from the Lord one day. But all the rest of the twelve Fol-lowed Je-sus all the way.

If You're Happy

TRADITIONAL

Happily

1. If you're hap-py and you know it, clap your hands (*clap, clap*). If you're

mf

hap-py and you know it, clap your hands (*clap, clap*). If you're

hap-py and you know it, then you real-ly ought to show it. If you're

hap - py and you know it, clap your hands *(clap,* *clap).*

2. If you're happy and you know it,
   Stomp your feet *(stomp, stomp).*
   (Repeat as above)

4. If you're happy and you know it,
   Stand up *(stand up).*

3. If you're happy and you know it,
   Shout "hooray" *(hooray).*

5. If you're happy and you know it,
   Do all four *(clap, stomp, hooray, and stand up).*
   (Repeat as above)

VARIATION
   Sing verse 1 as above.
   Verse 2: If you're sad and you know it,
            Tell a friend *(open and close hand with thumb touch-*
            ing fingers to signify speaking).
         If you're sad and you know it,
            Tell a friend *(repeat above actions).*
         If you're sad and you know it,
            Then you really ought to show it.
         If you're sad and you know it,
            Tell a friend *(repeat above).*

   Verse 3: If you're angry and you know it,
            Tell a friend *(open and close hand with thumb touch-*
            ing fingers to signify speaking).
         (Repeat as above)

   Verse 4: Repeat Verse 1.